SWANSEA'S HERITAGE

SWANSEA'S HERITAGE

RICHARD PORCH

Foreword by Iris Gower

First published 2008

The History Press Ltd
The Mill, Brimscombe Port
Stroud, Gloucestershire, GL5 2QG
www.thehistorypress.co.uk

Reprinted 2008, 2013

British Library Cataloguing in Publication Data.
A catalogue record for this book is available from the British Library.

ISBN 978 07524 4559 5

Typesetting and origination by
The History Press
Printed in Great Britain

Contents

Swansea

Nº VII.   *Cilfey old mill immediately over*

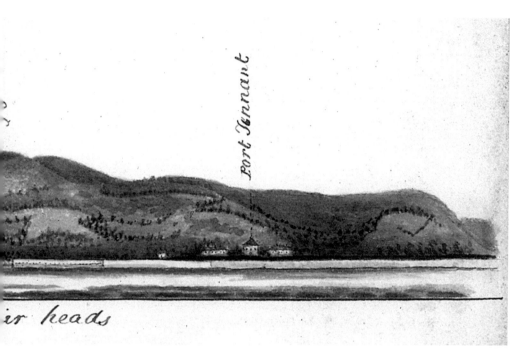

Port Tennant

ir heads

This view of Swansea was painted by Captain Martin White RN, who was employed as a member of the Naval Surveying Service and performed meticulous surveys of (among many other places) the Bristol Channel during the early nineteenth century. This view is taken from a Remark Book for the River Severn (UKHO ref. OD 190) compiled in 1823, while Captain White was commanding HMS *Shamrock*. This elegantly handwritten book includes sailing directions for ports and harbours on the Welsh side of the Bristol Channel. There is detailed tidal information, tables and a few coastal views such as this one. Captain White joined the Royal Navy in 1793 and retired in 1846, though his active career as a surveyor appears to have ended around 1830. He died in 1851. This image appears with the kind permission of the United Kingdom Hydrographic Office.

Acknowledgements

The geologists Dr Ronald Austin, Dr Eric Robinson, Dr John Davies, Dr Dyfed Elis-Gruffydd, Dr Geraint Owen of University of Wales, Swansea; Judith Porch for being so understanding, genealogist David Wiltshire for his help and guidance; Ken and Elaine Hughes of Trallwn Farm, Trallwn and Mair Williams for giving me permission to use an extract from the diary of Captain Dan Nicholas; the Conservation Section of the Planning Department, City & County of Swansea; the Central Reference Library, Swansea; West Glamorgan Archives, Mr Ken Attwell for giving me permission to reproduce extracts from his late wife Margaret's research on Captain David 'Potato' Jones; Mr Alan Price Roach for permission to reproduce the log kept by Benjamin Davies of a voyage from Mumbles to Chile aboard a Cape Horner; John and Joan Roach for allowing me access to their family-history research with regard to Harry and Benjamin Davies; William B. Harries Baker for his comments about Porthcawl; Gerald Gabb, Bernard Morris both of whom I regularly aimed questions at; Dr Gwyn Davies a retired physicist of Killay for permission to use extracts from his grandfather's works' journal; my dentist Mr Simon Jenkins in whose waiting room at Russell Street I conceived the idea for the counterfactual chapter; Mr Nick Mills for permission to use a photograph of North Dock in the 1930s from his collection; especial thanks to Commander Steve Malcolm RN of HMS *Scott* who introduced me to the work of Captain Martin White RN (17?? – 1851); Mr Colin Lamb for giving me permission to use the image of Robert Davies's gravestone in a Chilean cemetery; Katie Weston for assistance in researching Swansea in the 1870s; The UK Hydrographic Office (www.ukho.gov.uk) for permission to use the illustration by Captain Martin White RN; my thanks also to the Gomer Press for giving me permission to reprint an excerpt from Edith Courtney's *A Mouse Ran up My Nightie* (1975) entitled 'A Visit to Kilvey Hill'. If I have forgotten anyone else I do apologise.

Foreword

It is a privilege and a pleasure to write the foreword for Richard Porch's new book *Swansea's Heritage*. This is no 'dry as dust' book but a well researched, accessible history of our own area of Swansea, the place where I was born and have had the privilege of writing about for over twenty-five years.

Richard's research is sometimes anecdotal and happily his findings have verified my own; his tales of 'Mrs Evans the pee' and the story of Mr Clarke the ferry-boat man can be found in my own books and, as a novelist, a story teller, I am gratified to learn that an historian of Richard's calibre can confirm my rather less intellectual research.

The 'Swansea Miscellany' is a wonderful tool for the student or researcher in any field be it engineering or social science and is especially useful for any magpie writer who wishes to know how people lived in the 'old days.'

I have learned a great deal more about the area where I live from Richard's new book. The 'Urban Geology ...' piece I found fascinating and I loved the tales of the famous sea dogs who sailed from our port of Swansea.

I will be the first to buy the book when it is published, it will be embellished by photographs of Swansea and some of its inhabitants and of course I will want it signed by the author of whom I am a great fan.

Congratulations to Richard Porch on his wonderful new book.

Iris Gower

Introduction – An 'Erratic Compendium'

For the purposes of this book I have chosen not to start with the creation of Swansea in some distant prehistoric past and proceed chronologically toward its present. Instead I have decided to look at various elements that contributed to the creation of Swansea; namely the Vikings, ballast stones and how they got here and a geological walk through the city which will look at the building stones of Swansea. I will look at the lives of two notable Swansea sea captains of the Nineteenth and Twentieth Centuries and the lives of a father and son who each worked at the Upper Bank Copper Works and what they did with their lives. I have also included a purely speculative or counterfactual piece, to make the reader think a little bit about how Swansea might have turned out if the Industrial Revolution had been powered by electricity not steam. Finally, I have included a miscellany of Swansea's life and times from the twelfth to the twenty-first century. The idea here was to enable the reader to see via small nuggets of information, what went on in Swansea and the world it traded so successfully with. The net effect has turned out to be what the Swansea poet Nigel Jenkins called, in a completely different context, an 'erratic compendium'. It is one that will hopefully provide a multi-layered look at the history of Swansea from a number of different perspectives.

Bibliography

Intelligent Town by Louise Miskell
The History of the Port of Swansea by W.H. Jones
New Land for Old by Stephen Lavender
Historic Swansea by W.C. Jones/Bernard Morris
The Story of Swansea's Villages and Towns by Norman Lewis Thomas
Copperopolis by Stephen Hughes, Royal Commission for Historic and Ancient Monuments
The Buildings of Wales by John Newman, Penguin
The City of Swansea – Challenges and Changes by Ralph A. Griffiths,
The Industrial Archaeology of the Lower Swansea Valley by Stephen Hughes
The Lower Swansea Valley Project by K.J. Hilton, Longmans.
The Lower Swansea Fact Sheets Series by Swansea Museum
Swansea Castle and the Medieval Town by Edith Evans. Glamorgan–Gwent Archaeological Trust.

one

Of Vikings and Garden Walls

There is arguably no more tangential way of beginning a book on Swansea than in an unremarkable side street near the city's prison. Called William Street, it is separated from the Clarence public house by a street reassuringly called Clarence Street. For here you can see numerous garden walls ornamented by some ordinary-looking coping stones. These almost certainly replaced some late-Victorian or Edwardian wrought-iron railings of modest design removed at some point, presumably during the Second World War. Interestingly though, these stones do not originate from Swansea or even South Wales – so how did they find their way to a garden wall in the city? One possible answer is that they were deposited locally by 'glacial transport' – that is to say trapped in a glacier which inched its way down the Swansea Valley countless millennia ago. Or perhaps they came as ballast in the hold of some vessel.

Ballast is used when a ship which normally carries some sort of cargo is travelling empty and a substitute weight is needed to give it stability. This substitute cargo of ballast would then be dumped when nearing the port at which cargo would be taken on. Many materials were used as ballast: gravel, guano (bird manure) or most commonly, large stones. The key question is what sort of vessel might have carried these stones? A Roman trireme, a Viking longboat or a Victorian coastal steamer returning to Swansea with ballast, after having taken coal out? The rocks are interesting in themselves. They are examples of metamorphic (from the Greek meaning to change form) rock which is to say they were formed millions of years ago by the action of heat and pressure many miles below the earth's crust. Such was the heat and pressure that it has changed the original or parent rock (which may have been igneous or sedimentary) into a completely new rock called metamorphic gneiss. Gneiss is more often found in Scandinavia or Brittany than in Wales. Gneiss rocks are also the oldest in the UK and date from 2.7 million years ago. So how might these extremely venerable rocks have found their way to a garden wall near Swansea Prison? Finding stones not originally from Swansea in walls around the city is not uncommon. The same is true of those other once-great seaports of the South Wales coastal plain, Cardiff and Newport. You can see stones in the old walls of Swansea Castle that are not of local origin and were once conceivably ballast brought over by the Vikings. The 'Strand' (which means shoreline) ran below Swansea Castle and emptied into the River Tawe. Between 1845 and 1852 the North Dock was created by installing locks at both ends of a length of the river as it curved through the town. This created a 'floating dock' – one that was always full of water and not tidal. Bristol did this same thing in 1804, locking off a contorted stretch of the Avon as it looped through the town and adding a new stretch called 'the New Cut'. Forty years later Swansea too dug a new channel and this was also called the 'New Cut' and straightened the course of the river into the shape that we see today. So trading vessels coming up the river in, for example, the ninth century might have come to a stop at some primitive wharf on the Tawe virtually below the castle and discharged ballast which was later used in nearby building projects. It should be remembered that even in the medieval period Swansea had quite a large trading hinterland that included Ireland, England and France (Brittany). By contrast at the height of their powers the Viking trading empire stretched from Baghdad to Greenland and their coastal activities in the Irish Sea did not end until the reign of Elizabeth I (1558-1603).

A more everyday example of a metamorphic rock is that uniquely Welsh building material, slate. Slate is made from mud and silt deposits that build up on the sea bed. Over time this build up leads to the creation of shale or sedimentary rock. This build up went on over massive periods of time and, taken with an increase in pressure and temperature, caused a recrystallisation of the

A variety of stones are visible in William Street's garden walls all of which are probably ballast from one source or another.

shale's constituent minerals to take place. The result is called slate. You can see slate to the rear (south) elevation of the new National Waterfront Museum down in the Maritime Quarter. It was once silt on the bed of an ocean in the Cambrian Period, 500 million years ago. The slate used came from the Penrhyn Quarry in North Wales and there are two kinds used: a 'Heather Blue' and 'Heather Red'. A third was used called a 'Dark Blue Grey' and this came from the Cwt-y-Bugail Quarry, again in North Wales. Over 1,000 square metres of slate, 40mm thick, was used to clad over fifty pre-cast concrete panels, some of which weigh nearly 19 tons. If you now walk to the front of the museum and look at the floor surface to the right-hand side (as you stand in front of it) you will see more Pennant sandstone. This came from one of the few working sandstone quarries left in the Swansea Valley, on Gwrhyd Mountain. Notice this time that virtually every stone paviour has some sort of pattern to it. These are marks made by waves in a prehistoric river delta many hundreds of thousands of years ago. Not only that, you can see certain paviours bear the tell-tale marks of some bivalve (i.e. mussel) that had inched its way through the waterlogged sand of this prehistoric riverbed. Others bear the mark of a collapsed tunnel system crushed by being undermined or by a sudden inundation. Such marks are known as 'tracefossils' by geologists. There you have it – who would have thought that a thoroughly modern building like the National Waterfront Museum, Swansea would include either as part

The National Waterfront Museum Swansea, with its superb rear elevation in Welsh slate.

of the fabric of its building or as the paving around it, elements of the prehistoric past – but it does. This is a classic example of the fact that we see rocks and stones all around us and yet seldom if ever pause to reflect on what they are or where they come from; still less how they got where they did. Their story is locked forever in their apparently immutable form. We can find another story in the cladding of the Leeds Building Society in Union Street in the city centre. The stone panel or 'stall riser' beneath the main window is faced with Rapakivi Granite which was quarried in Southern Finland (*rapa* means mud or sludge and *kivi* means stone or rock) and its use forms part of the international trade in decorative building stones. It is also called 'Baltic Brown Marble' and is around 1,000-1,500 million years old and dates from the Proterozoic period. As you will doubtless appreciate by now, there is 'time' and there is 'geological time'. Ordinarily we think of a century as 'a long time', yet a piece of stone used decoratively in a shop front can have been around far longer than the dinosaurs. Yet because it is just some inert lump of coloured rock we waste no time in speculating about what its origins might have been in time or place. The Proterozoic Era began an unimaginable 2½ billion years ago and ended 543 million years ago. See what I mean about geological time? In this period the very first forms of life began to appear on a planet dominated by one large supercontinent called Pangaea. Britain was then located at the centre of it in an arid desert. These early life forms were actually nothing more complex than algae, bacteria and primitive multi-cellular creatures. Perhaps most importantly they were part of the 'building blocks of life', because they were pumping oxygen into a largely oxygen-free atmosphere. There was little ozone in the upper atmosphere and the planet was swept by the sun's harsh ultraviolet rays. If you envisage the evolution of life on earth as the sequence of letters in the alphabet then the Proterozoic Era is very much the letter 'A'.

We must return to those stones in the garden wall near Swansea Prison. The idea that they were once ballast is entirely plausible. After all, a drawing by Thomas Baxter of Swansea Ferry and Ty'r Llandwr Farm done as early as 1818 clearly shows ballast banks on the banks of the River Tawe. By this time Swansea Corporation had already designated space on the west bank of the river specifically to receive ballast from unladen sailing vessels. The unregulated dropping of ballast in the river had been going on for centuries and had begun to artificially silt up the river and cause obstruction to shipping. In fact there were regulations in place as long ago as 1555 to penalise the discharge of ballast into the Tawe. This is odd when you consider that good building stone was in real demand. The Pennant Sandstone of Townhill, etc. was considered too ' … soft, friable and flakey' (W.H. Jones). Stone used as ballast came from such disparate places a Waterford in Ireland and Bideford in North Devon. Nevertheless, I still cling to the idea that the Vikings may also have had a hand in matters. I do this because in the course of looking at some of these garden walls with some geologists I talked to the man who built some of them. His name was Mr Powell. Now the thing you have to remember is that the building of garden walls some forty years ago did not begin and end with a visit to the garden centre. You didn't just go there and choose the colour and type you wanted from a yard full of reconstituted stone slabs. Rather, you physically collected them yourself from the nearest available source. Now, forty years ago, car-ownership levels were a fraction of today's so our Mr Powell did not go down to the river in his Austin A40, collect a load of stones (from its tidal banks) and drive back to William Street. No, I'd have thought he would have simply picked up his wheelbarrow and gone down to the seafront (which is about 200yds from his front door) and collected stones from the beach. This, as he confirmed to me, is precisely what he did. Therefore, as the stones in his garden wall

A Rapakivi stallriser to a shop front on Union Street – one of the oldest stones in existence.

came from the beach, it is entirely possible they may have been discharged as ballast at any time during the last 900 years. In any case vessels coming into Swansea during its metallurgical heyday tended to come in full of copper and went out full of anthracite, patent fuel or coal. Ship owners tried never to send their vessels anywhere in ballast as you were paying wages without return. The ship owners of nineteenth-century Swansea would have been highly unlikely to send their ships anywhere unladen. The main defect with my admittedly more romantic idea of them being 'Viking ballast' is that the stones in the garden wall look as if they have been quarried. They have that unfortunate 'broken tooth' appearance which disfigures so many urban garden walls in the city. They look as if they have been minimally cut and shaped with some sort of building activity in mind, presumably walls of one kind or another. Now the Vikings would just have scooped up a batch of large stones from the nearest river or stream and lobbed them in to the bottom of their longboat. They certainly would not have bothered cutting or shaping them in any way. Such river stones also would have been water washed over thousands of years and would consequentially have a smooth, rounded finish. Perhaps some of the more rounded stones used in walls were washed down the Tawe by the river?

Whatever the veracity of the 'Sweyne's Eye' legend, there clearly was a Viking influence in the Bristol Channel area. Wales seems to have been spared Viking invasion until the middle of the ninth century which is surprising given that by then they already had bases in both

The top of the Guildhall clock tower with the Viking Longship emerging through all four sides.

Dublin and the Isle of Man. Their presence can still be detected in place names though, that other great repository of history, pickled as they tend to be in both local legend and municipal bureaucracy. Llandudno's 'Great Orme' is a good example of this; the latter word meaning 'serpent or dragon' in ancient Norse. They were presumably attracted there by the fact that the 'Orme' was once home to the biggest copper mines of the prehistoric world. Closer to home our own 'Lundy' is derived from the old Norse word *Lund*, the name the Vikings gave to the puffin. Fishguard originates from the Scandinavian word *fiskigarðr*, an enclosure for catching fish. Skomer comes from *Skálm*, the side of a cleft and was obviously the name given to a recognised coastal feature used as an aid to navigation. Interestingly *Llychlgnwgr* is the Welsh word for Viking and means 'people of the fjords'; it was first used in the thirteenth century. The English word 'Viking' only came into use as recently as 1808. It has to be said that there are killjoys around who will say that even some of the place names owe their origin more to immigration of peoples from the 'Danelaw' than an actual Viking presence in the region, the 'Danelaw' being those parts of northern and eastern England subject to Scandinavian rule which took place after 1066.

Nevertheless, given Swansea's natural geographic assets of a large, shallow bay and a tidal river navigable for several miles upstream, it is entirely plausible that the Vikings 'came, saw and conquered' Swansea in the name of adding to their Bristol Channel trading empire. It is important to remember that they were great traders as well as sea-borne warriors bent on the rape, pillage and plunder of legend. Swansea was only spelt the way we use it now as recently as the 1700s. Before that it was 'Swein' or 'Sweyn' which is surely significant. Local legend would have it that a Viking called 'Sweyn' sailed into the bay and up the river past a large island or sandbar that existed near where Fabian's Bay once was. Indeed, a reconstruction drawing by W.C. Rogers of Swansea as it might have looked in 1720 does indeed show an island at the mouth of the river with an 'Eastern channel' flowing around it. The island is described as 'Swansea Bar, a loaming gravel ridge, part of which still stood nine feet six inches above the pierhead's channel in 1824'. Legend has it that the island was known as 'Sweyn's Eye' and hence the settlement which grew up around it became known as 'Sweynseye' which gradually mutated into 'Swansea'.

The gradual mutation is interesting, for example in a twelfth-century Charter of William de Newburgh Earl of Warwick, to the Burgesses of Swansea it was spelt 'Sweynesse'. In a Charter of King John to the burgesses of Swansea of 5 May 1215 it is 'Sweyneshe'. There is a Charter of Henry II of March 1234 in which it is spelt 'Sweinesheie' and there is even an indenture dated August 1335 in which it spelt two different ways within the same document. Then it was spelt 'Swenseie' and 'Sweyneseye'. In a letters patent of Edward III dated February 1338 that last spelling was used again. By 1449 and in an account for the borough it had become the more recognisable 'Sweynsey'. A Charter of Oliver Cromwell in January 1655 made out to … 'the burgesses of Swansey' seems to more or less arrive at the modern spelling and pronunciation. We are now well on the way to the modern version which seems to be in widespread use by the onset of the eighteenth century.

As for actual surviving elements of the Vikings and Swansea these are non-existent. You will look in vain for evidence in terms of archaeology or numismatics (coin hordes). The Vikings appear to have made little impact on the Welsh language, political structures and left no visible remains of settlements. The legend still has the power to inspire nevertheless. When the architect

Sir Percy Thomas came to design the Guildhall in the 1930s he included Viking motifs in various decorative additions to the building. Apart from the decorative features used in the architecture of the Guildhall, look at the keystones to the entrance hall, the handrail to the main staircase and the clock tower which contains a Viking longship emerging from it.

If this has whetted your appetite for more 'Urban Geology', I have prepared a trail for you to follow which comes next.

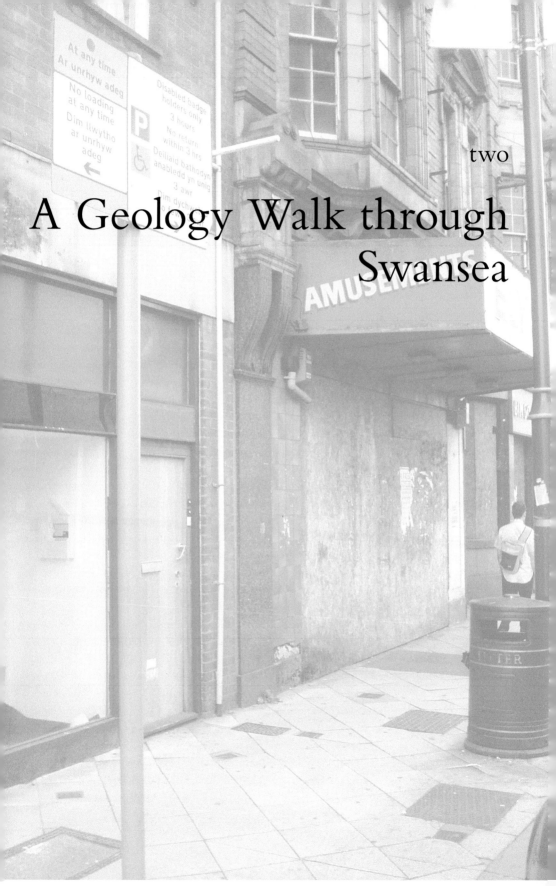

two

A Geology Walk through Swansea

When one thinks of geology, one tends to think of it as an activity carried out in wild and remote places. One thinks of people with rock hammers, rucksacks and walking boots attacking outcrops of weathered stone. In fact you can do quite a lot of geology in urban Swansea … if you know what to look for.

A combination of Swansea's own geology, the fact it has been a port trading with Europe since the 1500s and, taken with the nineteenth-century trade in building stone, ensures a rich harvest of geological material. The best way to discover the delights of 'urban geology' in Swansea is to give oneself a 'trail' to follow and here is one I have devised in the company of some eminent geologists who have taken me on walks through the city.

I suggest you start at a common point of arrival in Swansea, High Street Railway Station. Opened in 1850, it was the terminus of the South Wales Railway, of which Isambard Kingdom Brunel was made the chief engineer in 1844, although the station building itself that now looks out onto High Street is only a creation of the 1930s. It is made from a fossil-bearing Portland stone and if you look carefully, you can see fossil fragments embedded in it. One such can be seen to the right-hand-side walling as you leave the station and emerge onto the flagstones and bluestone paving outside the station. The way the stone has been cut has preserved it as a cross section through a prehistoric oyster. Proceeding down High Street in a southerly direction it is very easy to overlook the kerbstones, particularly those on the station side of the street. These are igneous rocks, ones that have had their internal composition changed by high temperatures and extreme pressure. There are a number of varieties of kerbstone and they include Gabbro, Diorite and Red Granite. All are coarse-grained igneous rocks formed by a cooling process deep within the earth's crust. The word 'igneous' originates from the Latin *ignis,* meaning fire. The origins of these kerbstones may well have been Brittany or the Channel Islands, many of the headstones in Oystermouth Cemetery may have this place of origin too. The Gabbro probably came from Guernsey and this stone was also used in the steps of St Paul's Cathedral in London. In a large number of instances you will see that certain kerbstones bear a dark black or deep blue mark. You might be forgiven for thinking that this was merely chewing gum congealed into place by years of pedestrian foot traffic. But no, what you are looking at is a geological phenomenon called an 'inclusion'. The local stonemasons, who were all nonconformists, colloquially called them 'heathens'. These were created eons ago when the rock began to melt at 900°C deep inside some mountain chain digesting the surrounding rock it as it did so. This caused portions of the 'country rock', as it is called, to become incorporated into the granite as a blotch or mark some of which are almost transparent now.

The very observant among you might spot something else about High Street's kerbstones. A fair number of them, especially towards the top end of High Street, sport a curious arrow-shaped mark. They appear on kerbstones in all sorts of positions and are not of a uniform shape or quality. When I first saw them I thought they must be Ordnance Survey bench marks, I was rapidly disabused of that idea. Anyway, these marks appeared exclusively in the horizontal plane – not the vertical. Then I thought they might be some sort of orientation mark executed by some long-lost contractor laying the kerbs in order to show which side faced out or in. However, the very randomness of their orientation gave the lie to that idea as they point all over the compass. A little more detailed research into stonemason's marks revealed that they were most likely made by individual masons to indicate to their foreman which individual had produced how much over a given period. Getting an individual to (literally) put his 'mark' on a series of granite kerbs enabled

This fossil can be seen in the Portland stone walling to the right-hand side of High Street Station as you leave it. It is thought to be a section through a prehistoric oyster.

the employer to do two things. Firstly (and most obviously) he could calculate how many kerbs this or that mason had carved which meant he could cost the mason's output. Secondly it enabled a significant degree of quality control to be exerted, especially since forgery was all but impossible. The stonemason's mark assigned responsibility and was in effect a trademark or signature. Such kerbstones had to be produced in large numbers as the town's streets grew in number. In all probability a production line existed with young or inexperienced masons crudely 'dressing' stones before passing them on to a 'master mason' to finish. For the master mason to demonstrate how many he had completed in a day and to what standard, he would have to mark them in some way. In addition there was absolutely no guarantee that the person who carved them could read or write. Such marks did not have to be ornate or artistic – after all you would not have wanted to spend much time on carving them. The ones on High Street are a long way removed from the kind to be seen carved into some medieval cathedrals or stonework to be found on the canal system. They were probably only there to facilitate payment and demonstrate quality. Mason's marks are as old as building itself and can be found on structures going back to 2,500 BC.

Moving further along High Street one sees the currently forlorn shell of the Elysium Building. Formerly the Rialto Cinema, a bingo hall and latterly the headquarters of the Labour Party in Swansea it is of interest to the urban geologist. This is because of a panel of black Larvikite in its frontage. Larvikite is a fine example of the international trade in building stone. It can only be

An inclusion or 'Xenolith' to be found in many kerbstones on High Street.

found in the Larvik district of Oslo Fjord, Southern Norway Often taken for a marble of some sort, it is another coarse-grained igneous rock containing highly attractive feldspar crystals that endow it with a depth that seems almost three-dimensional close up. Sliced thinly it is almost transparent and is thought to have first made its appearance as a facing stone in Germany in the 1890s. It is known in the stone trade by a number of picturesque names including Blue Granite, Norwegian Pearl Granite and (perhaps most facetiously) as 'Montague Burtonite'. The latter name refers to the tailoring firm of Montague Burton who in the 1950s and 1960s purveyed ready-made suits to a mass market in the UK. They used it extensively as a faux-marble on the facades of their branches all over Britain. The appeal of Larvikite was and is, that it looks like a luxurious marble but does not cost the same. In fact the term 'marble' means nothing more (at least to the stone trade) than any rock that will take and retain a surface polish. Larvikite covers the ground floor of Harrods in London and the famous explorer Thor Heyerdahl (*Kon-Tiki* et al) was born in Larvik.

Progressing further down High Street one soon meets Kings Lane. This unprepossessing and steeply sloping lane nowadays connects High Street with the surface parking of the Strand and the shops of the Parc Tawe shopping complex. I wonder how many people who use it to get to High Street every day are aware of how old a thoroughfare it is. Few, I'll warrant. For Kings Lane has also been known as King Street and Morris Lane and was once the line of the northernmost extremity of medieval Swansea's town wall. The North Gate

The former Elysium Club on High Street with a surviving panel of Larvikite in the centre of the photograph.

A stonemason's mark in a granite kerbstone on High Street.

entrance to the old town was where High Street is now. You can see what Kings Lane looked like in the 1850s from two watercolours by William Butler, to be found in Swansea Museum. He painted two views, one looking down it from High Street and the other looking up it from the Strand. It would have just been surfaced in dirt and cobbles at that time. The present building to the north side of the lane originated in the 1890s, it arouses mild curiosity because of the 'rake' or 'batter' of its ground-floor walls. By this I mean they slope outward like a form of buttress to support the weight of the building above. It was formerly Down's the Furnishers, whose shop faced out into High Street. It is not an old building as the highly detailed 1852 Board of Health plan does not show it, only a row of cottages. The walling to the south of the lane is of more interest because of the stones it contains. The lowest level of roughly coursed (laid in layers) stones have been cut and shaped as if for a wall. A number of people think this may well be a surviving element of the medieval town wall which led to the North Gate, although I have been counselled against declaring it to be so without archaeological evidence gathered via excavation. The smoother-shaped pebbles and stones above that lowest layer look like glacial material washed down the river or else a very early manifestation of our old friend, ship's ballast. As this lane decants out onto the Strand, which in medieval times was a bank of the river, the people who built the wall would have had

Kings Lane on High Street – its walls alone are a history lesson.

easy access to ballast dropped on the bank by traders from all over Europe; conceivably even Scandinavia or Brittany.

Moving further down High Street and crossing into Castle Bailey Street you soon see Castle Buildings. This large block was built in the 1930s and was severely damaged during the 'Three Night's Blitz' in the winter of 1941. It is of interest to the urban geologist because of the repairs done to it in the immediate post-war period which are still visible to this day. If you look carefully at the edges of the granite blocks to the openings of the various shop fronts, you will see what looks like a darker stone added to them. These are in fact repairs made necessary by the fire damage caused by the aftermath of enemy bombing. The heat from the burning building was not hot enough to melt the granite of its construction. It did however cause crystals in the outer part of these blocks to expand greatly. When doused with cold water on that freezing cold night in February 1941, the crystals contracted suddenly. Because the granite was made up of several minerals each with its own rate of cooling, the tensions between the crystals caused the minerals to become loose and fall away. The builders who restored Castle Buildings very cleverly used sand in their cement composed of the same minerals as the original granite. Nowadays the repair work resembles a 'scar' either to the edges of the blocks or even a 'blotch' to the 'face' of some of them. Immediately adjacent to Castle Buildings are the dramatic remains of what was

Post-war repairs show as darker stone on castle buildings which were damaged in the Second World War.

Castle buildings as they look today.

Swansea Castle, one of only two surviving medieval structures still to be seen in Swansea. As this is intended to be a short 'geology trail' this is no place for a highly condensed history of the castle. Instead what I would point out is that the north-east tower (nearest the Castle Cinema) is full of water-washed pebbles including 'schists' (metamorphic rocks with a leaved appearance) and red sandstones, presumably recovered from the banks of the river which once flowed below in the late thirteenth or early fourteenth centuries. Of course this is before the Victorians changed the course of the river in the 1840s by digging the New Cut in order to create the North Dock. The question of where the stones that Swansea Castle is made of originate from is the perennial one, of either Scandinavia or Brittany.

The outer fabric of the castle is faced with Pennant Sandstone conceivably from a quarry on Townhill with dressings of Sutton Stone, of which more later. You can see the old rubble core of the castle exposed on a corner exposed to Castle Bailey Street, which shows how the Pennant Sandstone covered the crude rubble core. An interesting feature can be found high in the wall of the north-east tower. If you face the castle, standing on Castle Bailey Street and look towards the well, on the left-hand side is a stretch of wall. At just above head height is a curious-looking stone that resembles a portion of carved stone, although no amount of close inspection will enable you to make out what it is. This stone is set into a wall made up largely of Pennant Sandstone and water-

An outer wall of Swansea Castle on Castle Bailey Street showing the older rubble core and many water-washed cobbles.

washed pebbles. It is not unusual to find material that has been 'robbed-out' of earlier buildings that have fallen into disuse and then been taken and used in a new building. Unfortunately more knowledgeable people than me assert that this likely-looking example of a robbed-out stone is actually nothing more than just the product of some mischievous weathering. Less contentious effects produced by erosion can be seen in the picturesque Green Dragon Lane. The stone to the pavement is the local Pennant sandstone while the kerbs, gutter slabs and the road cobbles are an 'exotic granite' from beyond South Wales. They probably came from Brittany or Scandinavia. The fascinating thing about this lane is the wear and tear to be seen in the road stones and the gutter slabs. You can clearly see where hand carts that have been pushed up the lane by generations of men have worn parallel grooves into the lanes road surface; you can even see where they have turned off right at the top of the lane to head up to High Street or the market.

Meanwhile in the gutter slabs is the evidence of heavier traffic, presumably iron-rimmed cart wheels. These, carrying much heavier cargos have worn clearly discernible 'ripples' into the granite over the last 150 years or more. Interestingly you can see this same sort of weathering to the granite road stones of the front part of Kings Lane next to the Kings Arms tavern on High Street. The origins of the name for Green Dragon Lane are unclear but can be speculated upon. You can see it on very basic property maps dating back to the mid-eighteenth century when it is simply called 'Green Dragon'. By the time of the highly detailed 1852 Board of Health plans it has become merely 'Dragon Street'. In the eighteenth century the lane emptied onto Padley's Yard which was on the Strand and which looked directly out into the river. By 1852 the river had been straightened into what was designated the New Cut and the original curved course of the river became the North Dock. This area and its immediate environs called the Strand became very much the province of the sailor and the dockhand. Accordingly many public houses sprang up to cater for them, one of which was called the Green Dragon, It was almost directly opposite where the Lane met the Strand. Other pubs immediately around it at that time rejoiced in names such as the Blue Anchor, the Tiger Inn and the Eagle. The Green Dragon was one of ten, all located within 100yds of one another on either side of the Strand.

Green Dragon Lane is flanked on one side by a former bank building with an ashlar frontage designed in a Greek Revival style dating from the 1930s, which is now a bar. On the other side of it is arguably one of Swansea's most elegant old buildings, the former head post office of 1898-1901. It was built by an architect employed by the post office called W.T. Oldrieve (1852-1922) in an austere but elegant style using a greenish facing material called Quarella Sandstone. This is an easily carved material which is susceptible to damage by weather erosion. Quarella Sandstone is mined in a narrow band that extends from Bridgend to Stormy Down in the Vale of Glamorgan. The name 'Quarella' is a corruption of the Welsh name for the area where the quarries were – 'Chwarelau'. Made of fine sand grains of quartz, it occurs in thick uniform beds that produce a consistent texture in all three dimensions. This made it ideal for use in buildings and for carving, as a result stonemasons called it a 'freestone'. As the name implies, this is a stone with a grain fine enough to be cut in any direction with saw, chisel or mallet. Unusually for the period this building also presents a strong elevation to Green Dragon Lane too.

Virtually opposite is a former branch of the Midland Bank. Built between 1908 and 1910 it was designed by the architect F. Adams Smith. This is an excellent essay in Edwardian public architecture and constructed in that great standby for work of this kind, Portland stone. Smith

A mischievously weathered stone to be found in the north-east tower of Swansea Castle to the left of the well.

Green Dragon Lane seen from the Strand. Ruts made by cart traffic can clearly be seen to either side of the central cobbles.

This is a detail of the paving in Green Dragon Lane showing the wear caused by wheeled traffic over 150-plus years.

makes the most of where the building leaves Wind Street and goes down St Mary's Street. At ground-floor level he curves the façade out and then at first-floor level recesses it before sending it out again at the level of the parapet. He then 'caps' the corner on the roof with a dome.

If you stay on that side of the road and carry on further down you come to Salubrious Passage. This is a marvellous curiosity piece, a passage at ground-floor level that takes you from Wind Street and carries you through to Princess Way. The buildings on either side of it date from the early 1800s. The 'Passage' cuts through on a structural wall which is supported at ground-floor level by squat cast-iron columns. The paving to the passage is probably Victorian and is of Pennant Sandstone. Emerging from the covered part of Salubrious Passage and carrying on down it, the very observant will spot a remnant of a fossil riverbed in the heart of Swansea. For, immediately adjacent to a hairdressers on the left-hand side can be seen some faint ripple marks in the one of Pennant Sandstone paving slabs. They are very faint but they are there. Generations of people over the last 200-plus years have trodden that passage never realising that they were walking on the remains of a prehistoric river bed laid down perhaps 350 million years ago. Salubrious Passage is a tantalising fragment of a Georgian 'court' and was one of many that must have penetrated both sides of Wind Street in that period. You can

The former head post office on Wind Street, its construction involved the use of many and varied building stones.

The former Midland Bank on Wind Street, now a bar, arguably the most attractive of all the former banks on that street.

Salubrious Passage on Wind Street, the surviving fragment of a late-Georgian court.

Ripple marks in a paving slab on Salubrious Passage, these were made 300-plus million years ago in the Upper Carboniferous Period.

see them on maps of the mid-Victorian period particularly well. They were an unhygienic invention and generated slums as densely packed houses sprang up around them. They must also have been a Godsend to criminals as they facilitated quick access and an easy escape once a crime had taken place.

Emerging from Salubrious Passage and turning right you will immediately discover Nos 2-4 Princess Way and the offices of Strick & Bellingham Solicitors. This delightful old building now looks slightly lost and forlorn as the city regenerates itself around it. Built in 1869 in the Gothic style, the architect was William Bacon Fowler. It is made of Pennant Sandstone with Bathstone cills and quoins. The Bathstone came from quarries at Box and Corsham in Wiltshire. The building is of geological interest because it is made of an Oolitic limestone which is riddled with the fossils of marine bivalves from the Middle Jurassic period that lived over 300 million years ago. This stone is easily carved but unfortunately it is also prone to weathering as the main façade of this building testifies. Capitals to the first-floor columns and the cills to the ground floor have been all but weathered out of existence due to acid rain. This lovely, but slightly down-at-heel example of Swansea's Victorian architectural heritage is destined to weather away in front of our very eyes. As the stone disappears grain by grain it also gives up the fossils trapped within it for millions of years. This is because the fossils are tougher than the surrounding stone they rest in and so stand clear of it as it flakes away. A poignant trade-off, I think you'll agree.

Strick & Bellingham Solicitors office on Princess Way.

Leave 2-4 Princess Way and follow the pavement up to the Cross Keys public house, the second of Swansea's two surviving medieval structures and the only one capable of being used. Although much altered in the seventeenth and twentieth centuries you can still see some fourteenth-century windows above and to the right of the main entrance. In the external walling can be seen numerous types of stone types ranging from Pennant Sandstone, Sutton stone and Bathstone. Apart from the Pennant Sandstone which doubtless came from local quarries, the others especially the rounded ones came from the river having probably been washed down from places like Penwyllt and Abercrave. Despite the many alterations done to it over the last six centuries, the Cross Keys still gives you a feel for how Swansea might have looked architecturally during the period 1500-1800.

If any of this has whetted your appetite, there is more to see. Proceed carefully from the Cross Keys public house into Castle Square and walk on towards the Kingsway. You need to walk up it until you see the NatWest Bank on the corner of Picton Arcade. The marble panels to its Kingsway elevation and the arcade are made of Devonian limestone from Belgium. These are 360-400 million years old and contain the fossils of a great many 'colonial corals' that can be seen in both section and longitudinally. So, the next time you pop into that branch or walk past in the arcade take a sideways glance at those panels. They are not just decorative – they contain the fossil remains of some primitive creatures that thrived in

A detail of the fossils embedded in a window cill of Strick & Bellingham Solicitors building.

a warm tropical sea millions of years ago. The panels are in effect a mineralised snapshot of them in their heyday.

Come away from that bank and proceed up the Kingsway until you reach Page Street and the delightful old Quaker Meeting House built in 1858. The walls surrounding it are comprised of our old friend, ballast stones. They contain chunks of gneiss, a metamorphic rock that is banded and coarse grained, containing alternate layers of dark and coloured minerals. Carrying on a short distance up St Helen's Road you will see a low, modern wall in front of the student accommodation building. Contained within that wall is a curious assembly of stones that looks as though the wall has been built around them. Given that St Helen's Road was one of the main roads out of Swansea to the west, it is entirely conceivable that what we see here is the remains of an old water butt or fountain. You can imagine travellers stopping to refresh themselves at what, even in the 1840s or 1850s, would still have been essentially a country road lined with only a few houses belonging to the gentry. This curious item appears to be made of both Sutton stone and Carboniferous limestone. The former is an early Jurassic creamy-white limestone. It is a freestone like Quarella that can be carved easily. Unlike Quarella, however, it is tough and resistant to weathering. It was widely used in South Wales from the eleventh to the sixteenth century and came from numerous small quarries on a hillside near Ogmore-on-Sea. It derives its name from a farm on the northern fringe of that seaside village. This curiosity is difficult to date but might be early Victorian.

A curious assembly of stones in a modern wall on St Helens Road – is it the remains of an old water butt or a fountain?

The Cross Keys public house, one of Swansea's two surviving medieval buildings.

This is a detail from a stone panel of Devonian limestone from Belgium. The circular features are sections through colonial corals some 300-plus million years old.

Proceed further on until you see the dramatic form of St Andrews Church, then stop. The twin lanterns of this highly distinctive church, which was paid for by Scottish drapers, can be seen from many parts of the city centre. As if to confirm the origins of this building you can see churches of a similar design in Glasgow, mostly dating from the mid-nineteenth century. However, I would direct your interest not toward the architecture of the church but to the stonework at its derelict entrance gates. For here are rich pickings for the urban fossil hunter. Firstly, take a look at the stone gatepost which has been fashioned from a limestone of the Upper Jurassic period. This means it could have come from the Vale of Glamorgan or the Cotswolds. Close examination reveals it has been cut from a bed of stone with very distinctive bands running through it. The bands seem to be alternately heavy with fragmented fossil shells – then free of them. Limestone is a sedimentary rock composed of the endless accumulation of fragmented shells. The shells are of marine gastropods (snails) with the balance made up of algae or corals. A detail of the gatepost shows one gastropod shell that has not fragmented irredeemably. It has not been possible to conclusively identify it however; I am informed that there are some 'tall-spired' gastropods that date from the Carboniferous Period. The banded appearance of the gatepost was probably caused by successive prehistoric storm events (cyclones or hurricanes) that caused the layering of each band via a rapid deposit. Each band may represent half a day's sedimentation. Think of it – you can still see the effect of a prehistoric storm on St Helen's Road.

The derelict limestone gatepost at St Andrew's Church which clearly shows the banding produced by successive inundations in prehistoric times.

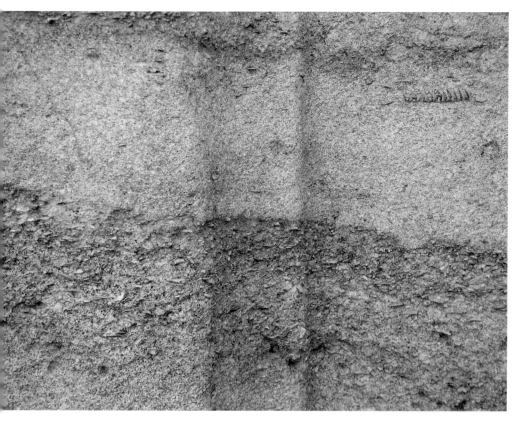

Banding to a stone gatepost at St Andrew's Church, denoting successive prehistoric inundations. Note the large marine fossil shell at top right.

If you walk through the non-existent gates you will see more Pennant Sandstone paving before you, leading up to the church itself. This paving is literally covered in ripple marks made by the ebb and flow of water on a prehistoric riverbed in the Upper Carboniferous period. Think of the countless numbers of worshippers who trod those slabs without ever realising they were walking on the remains of a fossil riverbed over which strode many exotic and now long-dead creatures consigned to evolutions dustbin. For sandstone such as these was indeed originally sediment on a riverbed. This can be demonstrated by getting hold of a piece and crumbling it down into a dust. If you do this you are left with the sand grains that constitute the original piece of sandstone – hence the name. The grains are bonded together by lime or silica and the iron oxides that endow it with its warm brown or orange hue. Sandstones tend not to bear the fossil shells of limestone, but they will show the burrows left by crawling creatures that lived inside it before it hardened over. On another level entirely, the very stone of St Andrew's Church itself has a story to tell. It is made of Bathstone, a middle-Jurassic limestone with a characteristic orange-brown colour. A traditional building stone of the Bath and the Cotswolds, the fact it can be found in Swansea indicates it arrived by train from some quarry in the West Country. St Andrew's was constructed between 1862 and 1864 and was designed by the architect Robert Dickson. Hence the use of Bathstone anywhere on a building in Swansea will automatically

Prehistoric ripple marks in the entrance paving to St Andrew's Church on St Helen's Road.

mean the building was built post-1850 and with the arrival of the railways.

Proceed onward now toward the Guildhall passing the remaining fragment of Alexander Graham's Swansea Infirmary of 1864 and cross Bryn-y-Mor Road. Pass by the Westbourne Hotel public house, a lunchtime watering hole of the author Kinglsey Amis in the late 1950s. If you look directly opposite the Westbourne Hotel across St Helen's Road you will see a red-brick building on the corner of Beach Street which was formerly a branch of Lloyds Bank (now a betting shop) where Vernon Watkins, the poet and good friend of Dylan Thomas, spent forty years of his working life. Redirecting our attention back to fossils and away from literary diversions, carry on up St Helen's Road until you find another of Swansea's 200-plus Listed Buildings in the form of St Paul's Church (completed in 1889) which has latterly been converted into an Indian restaurant called Miah's. At this point I was going to direct your attention to some limestone walling to the pavement where until very recently you would have found some brachiopod fossils from the Carboniferous limestone of Gower. Unfortunately the stones they were in became dislodged and were removed. This was a shame because the fossils were called productus and they consisted of two valves; a larger curved one which was heavy and a smaller generally flat one which formed a sort of lid. The animal lived in the space between. In one of the missing limestone rocks could be seen the shape of a productid shell left in the limestone (see photograph). That shape was made by a productid before it disintegrated. Another stone in that

A close-up of one of the productus fossils (in white) once to be seen in relief in the wall of an Indian restaurant on St Helen's Road.

wall (now also lost) contained the 'mineral ghost' of more productus, this time in relief. These must have been sitting together on the seabed when they were covered or died and their remains were briefly preserved in a wall outside an Indian restaurant. Who knows where they are now.

Continue now onward and up St Helen's Road until you see the impressive civic bulk of the Guildhall. Known to Swansea people of a certain age as The Civic, it was complete by 1938 and the design of the elevations (if not the plan) are very much those of a classical architect coming to terms with modernism. It is built in Portland Stone, of course, and there are plenty of fossil fragments to be seen pitting the walls to the right-hand-side, especially near the main doors to the entrance. The walls and the clock tower have 'entasis', a slope or inclination like that used on a classical column. It is deployed to counteract the optical illusion of an inward 'pull' as the building soars away from you in height. It is a delicate classicist's refinement of the architect Sir Percy Thomas. He gave the ground floor stonework a rusticated finish; this is one whereby courses of stones are left 'proud' of the rest of the building. Above that, the stonework is finished smooth except for framing to the windows and ledges to throw off rainwater.

The Guildhall is a good place to finish our urban geology walk through Swansea as it gives us an element of historical symmetry. If you recall, High Street Station was faced in Portland Stone too.

three

Two Stories of Swansea
Sea Captains

Cape Horner sailing vessels tied up in South Dock in the nineteenth century.

The ballast stones of Swansea and the men who manned the ships that brought them here have a tangential link to this next chapter. There is one Viking characteristic that has apparently survived in South West Wales and that is a love of the sea and of adventure. The countless West Walians and 'Swansea Jacks' who went off to sea in the nineteenth century to man the vessels bringing copper ore to Swansea were arguably Vikings in spirit if not origin. Therefore no book about *Swansea's Heritage* would be complete without recourse to telling the story of some of them. One such man was Captain Dan Nicholas (1844–1919) who was born at Tresare Farm, Pembrokeshire. Thankfully he kept a record of his life at sea between January 1858 and September 1904. This period, give or take a decade, was the apogee of Swansea's maritime-industrial success and so is of great interest for what it tells us about seafaring men and the lives they led. Dan Nicholas's 'short history' covers his forty-six years at sea and his ' … travels over the ocions', in his own words:

> My farther was a boy 10 years of age when the French landed at Fishguard. The heroine Jemima Nicholas who led the women and compelled the French to surrender was my great aunt ware her toom stone is now to be seen at the church yard Fishguard in memorial.

The French invasion of Fishguard took place on Wednesday 22 February 1797. It was comprised of 1,400 men who left Camaret led by an Irish-American called William Tate. This invasion force was a motley crew of ex-convicts and ex-soldiers, the cream of Napoleon's troops being

Captain Dan Nicholas.

Names	Births
Jemima Nicholas	1762. French invasion 1797 Jemima Nicholas died 1832
Evan. Nicholas	1791 at Tresare Pe...
Elizabeth Nicholas	1810 " "
Samuel Nicholas	Sept 25th 1845 at Tresare Pe...
William Nicholas	Sept 25th 1845 at Tresare Pe...
Annie Richards née Nicholas	March 23 1842 at Tresare Pe...
Ebenezer Nicholas	March 19 1838 at Tresare Pen...
Isaac Nicholas	Jan 24th 1851 at Tresare Pe...
Evan Nicholas	April 5 1849 at Tresare Pen...
Dan Nicholas	Jan 24th 1844 at Tresare Pe...
James Nicholas	Sept 22 1847 at Tresare Pe...
John Nicholas	Jan 17 1855 at Tresare Ten...
John, James Nicholas	July 29 1871 at Bristol
Elizabeth Ann Nicholas	Feb 20 1875 at Swansea
Evan. Nicholas	June 1 1880 at Swansea
Eugenia Williams née Nicholas	March 31 1883 at Swansea
Cecil Samuel Nicholas	Nov 5 1885 at Ynysmeu...
Idris. Nicholas	at Johannesb...
Herbert Cecil Nicholas	at Johannesbu...
Ivor. Nicholas	at Johannes...
Stanley. Muir. Nicholas	April 7 1920 at Ynysmeu...
Oliven Maude Nicholas	Feb 2 - 1922 at Johan...
Irene Myfanwy. Nicholas	March 24 1924 at Johann...

The family birth register for Captain Dan Nicholas; his name occurs nine names down.

Register

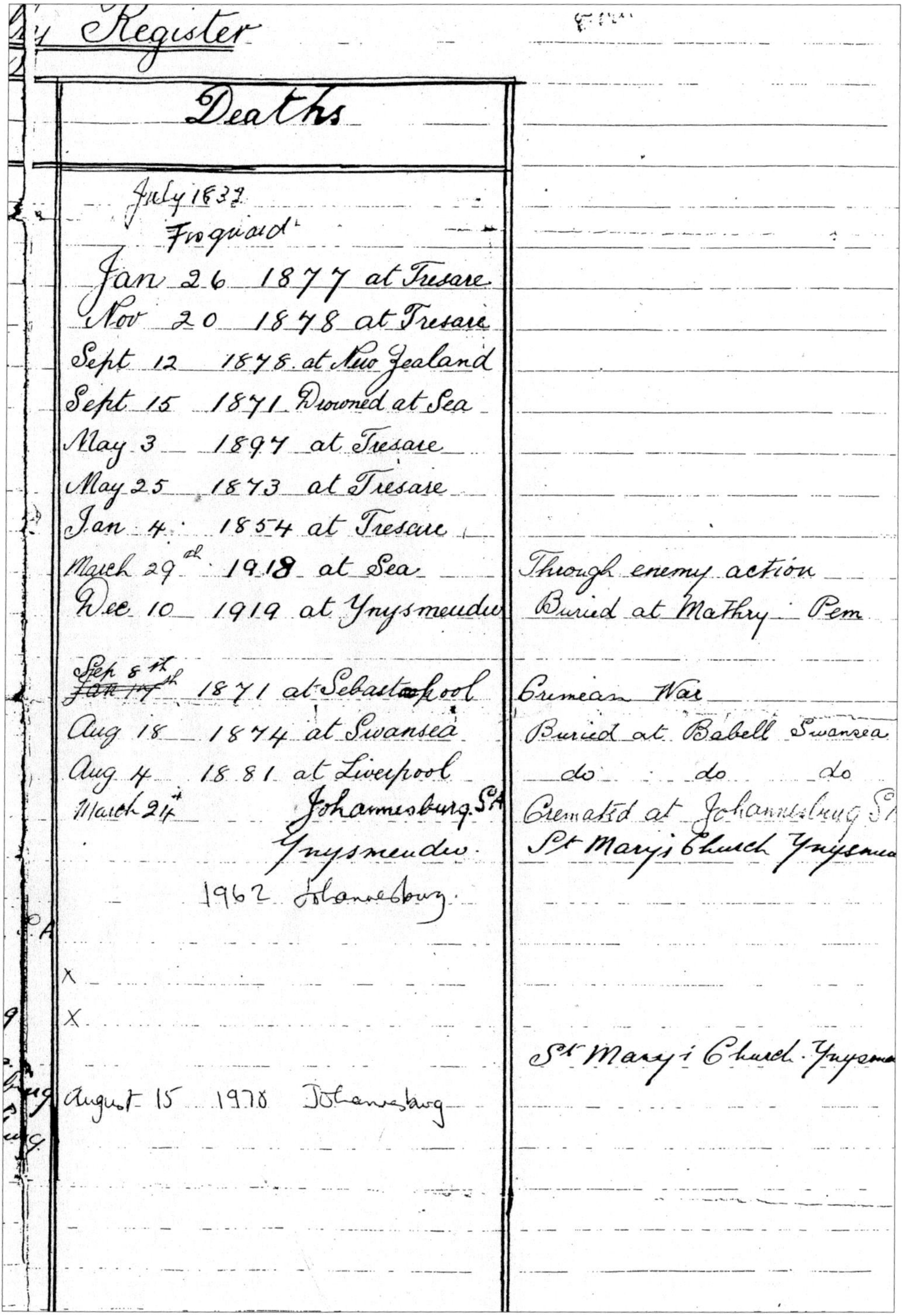

Deaths

July 1832
Frogiard

Jan 26 1877 at Tresare
Nov 20 1878 at Tresare
Sept 12 1878 at New Zealand
Sept 15 1871 Drowned at Sea
May 3 1897 at Tresare
May 25 1873 at Tresare
Jan 4 1854 at Tresare
March 29th 1918 at Sea — Through enemy action
Dec 10 1919 at Ynysmeudw — Buried at Mathry Pem

~~Jan 14th~~ Sep 8th 1871 at Sebastopool — Crimean War
Aug 18 1874 at Swansea — Buried at Babell Swansea
Aug 4 1881 at Liverpool — do do do
March 24th Johannesburg S.A — Cremated at Johannesburg S.A
Ynysmeudw — St Mary's Church Ynysmeudw
1962 Johannesburg

X
X
St Mary's Church Ynysmeudw
August 15 1978 Johannesburg

The other side of the family register for Captain Dan Nicholas, this time recording his death, nine names down, as 10 December 1919.

the Barque True Blue of Port Adelaide bound to cape Town our meal was nothing but smoke & fire she soon went down in two days we arrived at Cape Town and remained there three weeks had a board of trade Inquiry and was acquited with honor then took Passage to Plymouth in the Noram Castle After been home for few months I went Master of ——— for one voyage returned to Lpool with cargo Catin then three of us Mr Hooper Mr Davies and My self bought the Barque Charlotte then lying for Sale at Lpool she would carry about 640 tons we loaded for Buenosares and home with with Colin to Lpool we kept her mostly on on the River plate & Bahia Blanka trade & well after running her for 7 years we sold her to a Goole firm for £00 more than we gave for her and she paid 40 % during the 7 years we had her so she was a very profitable and lucky ship we were detained for 4 Months at Santos Brazels been a Block in the Port and tormond was sick our People daing like rotten sheep we came away with the Mate and myself of the old hands and it was very hard to get men as they were pretty well all dead the Prentice was sent to hospital from the Bar Second Mate also he died following day we left then for River plate and so glad to get away detained by Wellington elsewhere in Europe. Their plan originally called for a landing at Bristol, then a march into Wales and onward to Liverpool. The weather, so often a factor in thwarting invasions of Britain, intervened, and they were forced instead to make for South West Wales and Pembrokeshire. Arriving in Fishguard Bay they were immediately greeted with canon fire. The French were not to know it but this was only an alarm; nevertheless they retreated immediately and sailed on until they found a quiet sandy beach near Llanwnda. Here the French unloaded their troops and by the early hours of Thursday 23 February 1797, the last successful invasion of Britain had been completed. Their ships put back to sea and set sail for France. The morale of the troops and the quality of the leadership can only be guessed at, but after an initial looting spree in and around Fishguard the invasion collapsed as the troops became too drunk to fight. They surrendered to a local militia force on Friday 25 February. In the course of the 'invasion', Dan Nicholas's great aunt, the redoubtable Jemima Nicholas, the forty-seven-year-old wife of a Fishguard man personally captured twelve Frenchmen. Upon hearing of the 'invasion' she made for Llanwnda and confronted a detachment of the drunken and demoralised force and marched them into town before leaving to look for more. Jemima Fawr went down in history as a heroine. Similarly the explanation for the wholesale surrender of the invasion force was that they mistook local Welsh women in their native costume of tall black hats for British redcoats, also entered legend. Whatever it was – it worked and only the second successful invasion of these islands since the Battle of Hastings in 1066 was brought to a happy conclusion.

Back to Dan Nicholas's account:

My farther Evan Nicholas went to sea as Apprentice when about 13 years of age and when his apprenticeship had expired the ship was then at Cove of Cork which is now called Queenstown the Press Gang got hold of him the day his apprenticeship was out and he was takin on board of man of war ship and sailed for America as the Americans was claiming their Independance. He assisted in taking possession of the sea ports New York for one, then the sailors was landed and send into the bush or country to fight Washington's army. My farther was wounded, had recived two bulits in fleshey part of the leg and for years they kept on fighting but Washington was too much for them. After six years in the navy I beleave under Admiral Cockburn they ware, pease (peace) was proclaimed and he was liberated. Not many years after, my farther commanded a brig caring emigrants out to America and remained on that trade until he was 38 years of age, when his farther died and he took possession of the Farm, and when he was 40 years of age he got married to a young farmer's daughter 20 years of age and they had a family of 11 children 10 boys and 1 girl of which I am the 7 from marriage …

This seemingly dramatic change in career direction from farm boy to sailor then returning to the land was by no means unusual for this period.

Dan Nicholas:

Well now I am coming to my history. In April 1858 was made apprentice on the Barque Economist. For 4 years I was having £24 for the four years. There is 2 or 3 things happened while I was serving my time. We ware constantly on the American trades; first was I beleave for I have no dates the death of Prince Albert (1852). After arrival at Milford from Savannah S. Coast my fellow Prentice also died on board. The second is the taking in a cargo of cols at Llanely, every lump lowered in a bucket to ship hold. This cargo we ware taking out to St. John's Newfoundland to meet the 1st. present King Edward 4th. Who was then the Prince of Wales taking his first tower (tour) to America. Our coal was to supply the Men of Wars which was escorting him. Grand times at Newfoundland then.

Now, happening was the braking out of the Civil War in America or Slave War. We Ware then loading timber at Savannah S. Coast. We receaved orders to clear from port in 3 days so we just finished loading an sailed when guns was fired at Charlestown which we could distingly (distantly) hear. I used to go to the slave market at Savannah and seen them selling and buying. The buyer examined well something similar to what our cattle drovers are doing about Pontardawe … Well I remember the Gale of the Royal Charter. A fellow Aprentice was drownded that night. Well I secured my full Aprenticeship and was well pleased with my vocation altho' for many nights and days during my Aprenticeship I have been lashed with ropes to the Pump and pump, pump away never a lack, did not know the minite she would sink and we buried in the great Ocion. Then on the other hand we had gay times when the weather was fine and in ports and I felt proud of having gon through the dangers and perils of the deep in what they now call floating coffins, at present time such ships as I served my apprenticeship (in) wood not be allowed to leave harbour; 4 times I fell overboard once from the mast. Lucky ship no lives lost at sea during my aprenticeship. We had 5 cases of smallpox on voyage from Cardiff to Cape Verde and I was put to look after and attend to them keeping flais (flies) of them in the day and rats at night. Weather been very warm ship infested with rats. Captain was a good doctor got them all through it right anough (enough).

Next voyage in this ship (Brigantine called Primrar) was from Cardiff to Alicant Meditranian and Pameran (Panama?) to Bristol. Copper ore then to Llanelly. I left and went home for a few weeks. I then joined a ship called the N----- of Ged---- on the French trade. After sailing we had a heavy storm went into Mumbles Roads until finer weather came and proceeded to Bordeaux in France and returnd in ballast to Llanelly. The owner was a coal merchant and a Frenchman. Loaded for Q----- west of Lundy Island in thick fog. Got foul of a French vessel, carried away his mast and also our topmast. We proceeded on but ship had been very leaky … at the pump the whole time. We got into Steve's bay and ordered 8 men had -----engaged to pump until haigh (high) water next morning. We sailors was real fagged out. The mate was no good pretending to be sick and did not help. The water was over the forecastle struts but I slept soundly until I heard the cable chain running over my head. I rund on deck found they had slipped the cable and running in for repear and they ware all of them more or less drunk. They had found brandy jar in cabin and emptied it. Captain had his wife and baby on board. When tide left the ship we found the leak and stoped it. The mate left the ship and not great loss and again sailed. I was now promoted Mate again sailed for Llanelly and in due time arrived back in France … Then I joined the ship Humber and went to Bombay. Good discipline on board this ship. Captain was R.N.R Was 6 months going out, from there went to Calcutta for repairs as she had sprung a leak coming out. Cholera was very bad. At Calcutta several of the crew died and the rest paid off and I was one man shipped on the Enturpe bound to London. This was a large iron ship at that time she would carry about 3,200 tons. Bad luck began on first movement of this vessel. Dropping down the Ganges clear of this I -----chain cable hook charges and rund out to b-----end all castings of windlass smashed up. Got her holed to Colle Bazari moorings below Fort William in 10 days windlass was fixed and towed down the river to sea when tug and pilot left the ship. 2nd day out, a young man died with cholera and one after the other kept dropping every day. Then the news came that the captain was bad. Chief mate had been laid up for days so 10pm following night the orders came all hands on deck, take in sails. It did not blow but we thought that the officers anticipated a cycalone coming. The sails was soon reduced down to storm sails then all hands was called aft to get grog. After having our rum we ware informed that the captain was dead, for 4 of us to come into the cabin to carry his body on deck. I was one that helped to carry him. I put my two hands under the back of his head while 4 others was lifting his body. His head fell back and his eyes wide open staring one in the face. I nearly fainted. The body was warm and quite supple with heavy perspiration. The body was put upon the poop deck and covered with a sheet. That night was the longest two hours ever I spent at ship wheel alone on the deck with corps (corpse), wind blowing the sheat (sheet) I kept thinking that the body was moving to get up. The second mate took plenty of drink and kept off the poop. Following morning at 8am the funeral took place, steward reading the burial prayers and the body of the strong man was committed to the deep. As previously stated, the Chief mate was laid up since we left and he did know of capt'n death. Now the ship was at the mercy of the wind as we had no navigator on board, the 2nd mate already alluded to was no navigator. He had been promoted from bosun to fill a second mate position. He could not read. Now the steward and him had full charge. Steward had predicted that the Chief Mate's case was hopeless it was only a matter of time he would follow the others, but in about 10 or 12 days the Chief began to revive and becoming stronger daily with assistance to come on deck he was able to take observation and soon came to know ship's position and he grew fat and strong. Now we had 6 to 8 laid up yet with acute daiarey (diarrhoea). We called off Asention (Ascension) Island for mail and medicin and kept backing and filling for the most part of the night waiting for the new captain to come on board. He went strite to his bed and all hands, Second mate included with exception of a black sailor and myself they ware all drunk and fighting. Got ap--------on one mast square and the black sailor steared through and at brake of day I went to releave him and as I was goaing aft there was a terrible sight along the decks. Cook was laying by the galley door with his big toe hanging to a piece of skin in a pool of blood and sailors here and there laying down full of cutts and bruises but worsed than all our second mate was laying there at the front of the poop with empty wisky bottle by him. This was the kind of man we had to trust our lives to. Things went farely well after everybody recovering we took T-------- of South Fr---land and made all sails fast. One of the sick men had died his body was taken ashore at Gravesend. By goaing up London river we collided with ship and a barge sunk s------------- we done damage to extent of four thousand pounds. There ends one of the most unfortunate voyages. Owners gone bankrupt and no wonder it is enough to brake the bank of Don Carlo … Last voyage we ware nearly shipwrecked in bay of Jrindy on St. Mary's island went againsed the rocks in foggy weather had her off but her bow was broken we ware loaded with general cargo mostly liquor in casks and sugar it was those casks that kept her afloat as she was half full of water eventually we got her into St. John's discharged and repared loaded deels for Newport then to Bristol dry dock to have thorough repares and coper (copper) put on her bottom than I left her then I shifted my residence from Bristol to Swansea than I joined the Burry as mate was in her for about two years on the Capleary Sardinia trade lead ore then I joined the Marian made a voyage to Baltimore and back to Tyne with corn had my fourth finger cut off in her. Left her in Tyne went home to Swansea and joined the ship Vain was in her for 8 months left her and took command of a new vessel called Elmira of Swansea this was in 1875. First trip was very successful Cape Verde Islands off St Jago loaded at Mayo salt for Rio de Janiero. Ordered to Santo to discharge. Went up to Bayhia loaded suger for Falmouth for orders. Ordered to Holland Roterdam I lost steward at Santos with yellow fever fine Christian young man. Came from Roterdam in ballast to Swansea well suffice to say that I was master of this ship for 9 years Brazil trade mostly. I lost several hands each trip at Santos by yellow fever and one voyage lost all hands except self and aprentice boy this boy was on board by himself for 6 weeks when I was in hospital with the fever. I left this ship at Pernambuco and came as passenger ill. I put a young man in my place. After been home a few months I went 2nd mate of steamer Stanmore on the tin trade Swansea to New York. On the 2nd voyage I got ship mate and stayed in her about 14 months as I could see no chance of getting promotion I left her at Swansea and took command of the City of Asaph I took quarter of her well I made a couple of voyages in her and the third voyage loaded coals for Port natal S. Africa we had rather long passage to the equator and going down the coast of Brazil found that the coals was on fire so we did not pump her for 48 hours and as the fire was at the bottom the water put out at least we thought so. Everything went alright for a few weeks but as were getting south and having bad weather it again lightedup (lighted up) and as we ware rowing for cape Good Hope it came unbearable no one could go below deck we tried all ways to keep it under but it kept growing now blowing a gale and high sea we ware steering in for Mossel bay when in the night she blew up her hatches and fire as high as her truck but only for a few seconds it was the accumulation of gas. At day light we saw a ship standing out from the land and we made cleare to her and asked them to put boat out and fatch (fetch) us as the ship was on fire Captain answered that their boats could not live in the sea so we hove the ship to and got our boat out with great difficulty and risk all got safely into the boat and pulled clear of the ship sea running mountains high in one hour got safely on the barque True Blue of Port Adelaide bound to Cape Town our vessel was nothing but smoke and fire she soon went down. In two days we arrived at Cape Town and remained there three weeks. Had Board of Trade enquiry and was acquitted with honor.

You can see from this account how cheap life was and the often scant regard for it that employers had. It was a world where everyone was trying to get away with what they could and the devil could take the hindmost. People died or were maimed at regular intervals and there was little or no redress. They had a Board of Trade enquiry for the loss of the vessel but would they have looked into the death of any sailors? One thinks not, they would simply have been wrapped in a shroud and dispatched to 'Davy Jones's locker'. Needless to say there was no doctor or ship's surgeon on board these vessels. How would his presence have been justified economically, other than being a doctor what could he do? Medical assistance, such as it was, was rendered by either the captain or the first mate and the quality of it was directly related to what they knew. Granted, most vessels carried some sort of medical manual but there was absolutely no guarantee that anyone could read it. Needless to say any medicine chest aboard would only have carried splints, bandages and sundry patent medicines.

Antiseptic material for cleaning wounds and so forth would have been conspicuous by its absence. The quality of medical care was erratic and largely of a do-it-yourself nature. After the above incident Dan Nicholas became part owner of a barque (the *Charlotte*) and plied a successful trade for seven years on the River Plate and Bahia Blanka trade. She was sold to a German firm for £200 more than was originally paid for her; he went on to be the master (captain) of numerous vessels and had many more adventures. By 1909 and at the ripe old age of sixty-five, Captain Dan Nicholas could record this in his diary:

In March 23rd 1909 I again went to Antwerp to put captain Griffiths out of Andorinha and remained there to superintend the repares of her for three months when she was sold to the Frenchman then came home and worked hard on the farm, (Tresare) which had been neglected.

Another brilliant account of life at sea in the nineteenth century was compiled by the late Margaret Attwell. Previously unpublished it was prepared with full access to the papers of one of Swansea's most colourful sea captains, Captain David 'Potato' Jones (1871-1962).

Margaret Attwell:

David John Jones was named after St. David by his Christian parents. Not a very apt name for someone who was so unsaintly. The name, "Potato Jones" came many years later. Young David was always quick volunteering to deliver finished suits and uniforms to the captains in the North Dock (his father was a tailor). Although only ten minutes walk away David would be gone for several hours.

He loved the ships and listening to yarns told by the crews. They would lead him on and tell him of the beautiful sun-drenched islands far away in foreign lands with swaying palms and pretty naked girls where he could live for a penny a day. But they never told him of the yellow fever, malaria, scurvy or being wet and cold for days on starvation rations. Neither could he have known of the dangers he would encounter during more than 50 years at sea.

David hated school especially during sunny days. He would miss school and ride his rickety bike down to Mumbles and sit on the headland that looked over the Bristol Channel. From there he could watch ships under full sail returning from some magic country far away. His parents gave up trying to stop him and the "Boardman" was a regular caller to his home. Threats from his parents or school had no affect at all. If it was a nice day or a ship he knew was leaving Swansea, he would be perched there like the statue at the entrance to Copenhagen harbour. Like all school children, he was often short of money. New ideas to earn a few extra pennies were always in his mind. One method was to dive under a moored ship. He would be under for ages and even some of the hardened crew would show concern. Whilst the crew looked over the side of the ship for him to surface, he would climb up the other side and scramble like a monkey up the rigging to the top of the mast. They would give him farthings or even half pennies for his antics. Sometimes they would give this ten-year old boy swigs of gin.

After threatening his parents that he would run away to sea, they finally gave in. On 16th March 1883, when just fourteen years old, David and his father went down to the docks so he could sign on as an apprentice. His first ship was the "Mary Rose". It was a three-masted barque of about 600 tons registered (tiny by today's standards). David was over the moon, as it was one of the ships he had admired as it stormed up the coast under full sail. It was also one of the ships where he used to sit on deck while listening to the yarns when it was docked. Like all sailors, he had a great send-off.

Over seventy years later he would recall with some emotion, the feeling of excitement he felt as the ship was slowly towed down the river at the top of the tide that late spring evening. He watched the lights of his lovely town disappear behind. Over the stern he saw the Mumbles Lighthouse blink as the ship sailed gracefully down channel to pass between Lundy Island and Hartland Point during the early hours of the next morning.

Within a few days he realised that the apprenticeship contract his father had signed was a contract for slavery. It stated, among other things, that he was to obey orders promptly without question at all times. The captain was very hard and David's tender age didn't matter, he was a man at fourteen!

His wages were £5 for the first year, £8 for the second, £11 for the third and £16 for his fourth and last year. This came to £40 for four years of what amounted to hard labour. His Able Seaman's rate would be £25 per annum and that would include rotten food, dirty water, hard tack that broke your

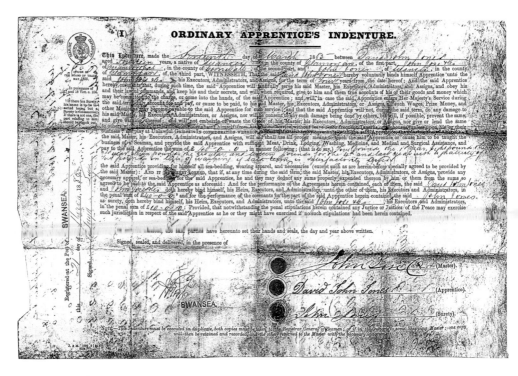

Potato Jones's Ordinary Apprentice's Indenture, dated March 1883.

teeth and sleeping under leaky decks that made your bedding wet and kept your clothes constantly wet or damp.

Out of his first year's wage, most would be taken by the detested "crimp". The "crimps" job included supplying the seaman's equipment and providing crew to captains who could not find them. Most of the money handled went into the crimps own pocket and what he supplied was of very poor quality. Although hated by all, the crimp served a useful purpose. By handling money in the form of vouchers, it prevented seamen taking wages and jumping ship as it was about to leave port. Many captains could not obtain crew, because of their reputation as slave drivers. The 'crimp' would arrange to "persuade" able-bodied men from local dockside pubs with the aid of large cheap gins, a wooden club, a few thugs and a hand cart.

Within a very few days young David was disillusioned. He was not prepared for the bullying and cruelty that was part of everyday life at sea. When an order was spat out and David was slow to respond, he would feel a knotted trope across his backside. Being a young apprentice meant he was a skivvy to all …

His first experience of the (Cape) "Horn" almost made him an instant Christian. Sailing east to west means against the current and the huge seas. He said during his first trip they had to tack for three weeks to get around the Horn. After fighting the seas day and night they could end up back where they had started the previous day. What a way to spend his 15th birthday. The weather was so bad they had to stand well out to sea. Too far for him to catch a glimpse of Cape Horn on his first trip.

There was no rest for anyone when rounding Cape Horn. It was all hands on deck and man the pumps to stay afloat. Wooden boats leaked badly when hard pressed and sometimes the caulking would shake out. David was very seasick for days and felt that he was going to die. There was no lying in bunks for him or anyone else.

After three months at sea they sighted land for the first time off the entrance to Valparaiso. He thought this was brilliant navigation. He and all the crew were desperate to get their feet back on dry land once more. But after three months at sea they were not allowed ashore. Valparaiso was a very busy port. Up to a hundred ships from many countries would be waiting for days outside the harbour before unloading.

Eventually a longboat would tow the ship into its berth. The captain and his chosen few would go ashore in advance to make arrangements with the resident agent to unload the cargo of steam coal they had shipped out from South Wales. They would row back at night drunk as lords. My grandfather said, 'It was the only time I saw the captain smile'.

If there was any delay in arranging a return cargo of copper ore, or any other profitable cargo, most of the crew would be laid off ashore without pay. It would be up to the crew to find their own accommodation or sleep rough. If the captain didn't like a crew member he would be paid off and have to find his own way back on another ship. He could wait for weeks in that "hell hole" full of prostitutes, thugs and murderers.

You will appreciate that terms of dismissal and opportunities to take an employer to an industrial tribunal are very much a modern convenience.

It worked both ways of course because a seaman could jump ship if he didn't like the captain and sign on to another ship for the return journey home. As there was regular trade between Swansea and Valparaiso a good seaman, cook or carpenter didn't have to wait long.

Margaret Attwell:

'Potato Jones' would repeat this tale of a notorious Swansea captain who sailed his boat loaded to the gunwales for a maximum share of profit. He had previously lost a ship and some of its crew and his license was withdrawn for only three months as a result. No-one wanted to sail with him so he was desperately short of crew. He contacted the 'crimp' and arranged for 6 able-bodied men to be supplied urgently at a dollar a head. He was fully-laden and ready to sail and being charged berthing fees by the day. The cost of berthing fees was eating into his share of the profit. The captain made a deal with a local 'crimp' (of whom it was said that he would sell his mother for a dollar) to supply six able-bodied men that same night. Sure enough six men were duly delivered by the 'crimp' and his thugs and dumped in the hold to sleep off their poisonous dose of gin.

In those days hygiene was not a strong point among seafaring men. So the scene next morning was of unwashed bodies in smelly clothes slowly coming to life in a dark, damp and dirty hold. The effects of cheap gin, concussion and sea-sickness usually meant they awoke to a coating of each other's vomit, urine and worse. The smell wafting up when the hatch was lifted next morning could be overpowering however on this occasion it was even worse. One of the press-ganged men had been dead for days. The captain was livid, not only was he one crew member short, but worse 'He'd paid a dollar for a dead man!'

The return trip was much faster than the outward journey, taking about 75 days as the seas and winds were usually favourable on the return journey. He couldn't wait to return home and tell his old school chums and parents about his adventures. They stormed up the Bristol Channel at good speed with all sails set. He knew how it must have looked; he had seen this same ship and others being driven hard the last few miles home in the past.

The 'Mary Rose' was towed upriver by a steam tug. A small weighted line was thrown ashore to a man at the entrance to the lock gates. This was used to haul out a heavier warp that was passed around a hydraulic capstan and sheaves that still exist at the entrance to South Dock. They were warped (hauled by ropes) into their berth and safely tied up. He made return trips about twice a year for the next four years to Chile and sometimes Cuba where there were small finds of copper ore. Occasionally they would be loaded with Guano (dried bird droppings) from Valparaiso. Guano was gathered from extremely dry deserts where rain had not fallen for hundreds of years. It was used as fertiliser on the farms all over Gower and the Vale of Glamorgan.

David was now a hardened seaman at seventeen and was entering Santiago in a ship he loved, the 'Margaret Ann'. Its captain and 1st Mate had gained his respect and loyalty. Although slave drivers they were true masters of their trade in every way. They took that little ship through terrible weather and horrendous seas. She was a fine Swansea "trunk built" ore ship. It was seaworthy and fast (about 15 knots) and would outpace any steam cargo ship in a fair wind. He felt safe in that wonderful vessel and loved everything about it from stem to stern. When all sails were hoisted and pulling hard in a fresh breeze it was majestic in the way it would plough through the sea.

I should explain the term 'trunk built'. Iron-ore vessels were often laden almost to deck level as there was no 'Plimsoll line' to limit the tonnage carried. Extra tons meant extra profit. As a result, decks were often awash even in moderate seas. Pumping out just to stay afloat was a part of everyday life. Copper ore was a mixture of ore and dirt. If water sloshed about it would form a slurry and movement would wear the hull and frames from within. Wooden trunks similar to large coffins were supported and fastened away from the planking and were fixed above the hull's frames to spread the load evenly along the length and breadth of the hull. Sufficient clearance between the hull and underside of the trunks allowed the ship's carpenter to crawl into the filthy bilges and inspect the structures. A clearance under the trunks ensured that the bilge-pump inlets wouldn't be blocked by slurry. This construction also allowed other loose materials to be shipped such as coal and limestone. What the trunk did was to effectively raise the ship's centre of gravity. Having a very dense cargo such as copper resting at the bottom of the ship (and liable to shift in heavy weather) meant the vessel could be dismasted in rough conditions because of the strain imparted by the heavy cargo on the rigging. No wonder that sailors of the period thought they could hear the ship 'moan and groan' when taking a pounding in adverse weather. The trunk began to be fitted in the 1840s. This was before Swansea had built any docks and ships had to tie up at mooring posts sited along the river banks. Some of these posts can still be seen today – there are some near New Cut Bridge on the west bank. This posed problems for heavily laden copper-ore vessels due to the extensive (pre-barrage at least) tidal range of the Bristol Channel, which could play havoc with an already hard-worked ship's structure. A heavily laden copper-ore barque laid aground on the bed of the river at low tide was under a lot strain even though technically not at sea. Copper ore did not – unless trimmed when being loaded - settle evenly so consequently loads could be unevenly distributed. The 'trunk' also brought with it other benefits in that it worked to 'insulate' the cargo from the fabric of the vessel. One potentially disastrous side-effect of carrying copper in the hold was that it caused corrosion of the iron bolts holding the vessel together. It did this because copper salts were leeched out by salt water leaking into the hold. These Cape Horner's although fast were far from watertight. The action of this resulted in the iron being dissolved and replaced by an unstable mass of copper. This would, unless rectified, result in the planks on the ship's hull falling away admitting the sea. Three warships were lost in the War of Independence with the Americans (1775-1783) in this way. They were experimenting with sheathing the hulls of vessels with copper as long ago as the 1770s and did not know about the chemical reaction between copper, sea water and iron bolts.

Margaret Atwell:

Life aboard didn't improve much, the relationship between crew and skipper was still like slaves and master. The whip was part of the ships inventory though never used on the 'Margaret Ann. But the knotted end of a rope was used on crew members the 'old man' thought were too slow. Often the most effective weapon for discipline was the first mate's fist. To retain respect it was essential to be handy with their fists and heaven help the man who gave 'lip' to the first mate.

As they approached Valparaiso harbour David noticed three unmanned barques at anchor, each flying a yellow flag from their rigging. It was a warning to all that they had yellow fever aboard. A sight he saw both in Chile and Cuba. Often these vessels were Swansea registered because in the 1880s there wer more than 500 Swansea vessels trading around the world, it was common to meet with other Swansea registered ships in foreign ports. The name 'Abertawe' was never carved into the stern of any vessel because the international language, then as now, was English. But he saw the name Abertawe several times carved on crosses (in graveyards) in Santiago, Havana and other ports – victims mostly of yellow fever!

Yellow Fever or 'Yellow Jack' as it was also known, was no stranger to Swansea either as outbreaks occurred in Swansea during 1865 and 1866. It also worked the other way too, not for nothing was Santiago known as 'Swansea Cemetery'.

Margaret Atwell:

Swansea could be identified from well down the Bristol Channel even before reaching Lundy Island by the black cloud of pollution that hovered over the town in the 1800s. There were over sixty foundries, tinplate mills, steel works and spelter plants in the Swansea, Neath and Llanelli area. Pollution was terrible and the air was filled with sulphurous fumes day and night. Despite this (David) loved his home town and was always excited when he entered the bay even if it was only for a twelve-hour turnaround time.

During his time on the 'Mary Rose' and the 'Margaret Ann' he studied at every opportunity with help from the 1st mate and 'The Old Man' (as captains were known). David became an 'Able Seaman' by 1889. During 1890 and 1891 he had his first experiences on steamships named 'The Potomac' and the 'James Drake' trading between Cardiff and the Black Sea. He found their motion unpleasant after the steady motion of sailing ships. Throughout his life at sea he always suffered from seasickness for the first few days, so the hot smell of steam engines didn't help.

At first he didn't like steamships much. He said they "rolled like pigs" especially when in ballast (unladen). They were slow but reliable and over short passages could work to a timetable, unheard of in sailing ships. It became obvious that the days of sail were numbered.

In 1892 he was back into sail again and set sail in the barque 'Delta'. He obtained his Second Mate's ticket on the 'Hinda' and his First Mate ticket in 1903 on the 'Zadok'. Both Swansea trunk-built sailing ships.

Potato Jones's Certificate of Discharge dated April 1890.

The *Hinda* was an iron barque of 476 tons gross or 700 tons deadweight, owned by Simon Goldberg, a Jewish ship owner from Swansea. It was launched in 1870 and usually carried patent fuel on the outward journey from Swansea and semi-refined copper ore from Chile on the homeward run.

Margaret Atwell:

From 1904 onwards David Jones sailed only steamships. They traded from Cardiff, Barry and Swansea to many foreign ports including the Mediterranean, the Black Sea and European ports up the Baltic. On 27th August 1909 he gained his master's certificate (no 005304). The following day he was presented with his certificate of competency for foreign-going steamships and endorsed for square-rigged sailing ships. Within a week he became master of his first vessel the 'Cymrian'. By this time he was married with four children and living in 23 Park Place, Brynmill. Although during the next 30 years they saw little of him as he was away from home for up to a year at a time. He soon became familiar with most Mediterranean ports and was allowed to enter and leave many ports without the need of a pilot aboard his ship, a fact he was very proud of. I have spoken to crew who sailed for my grandfather and they told me how ruthless he was. He seldom allowed

Potato Jones's Certificate of Discharge dated November 1900.

his crew ashore in case they jumped ship. He kept the crew busy painting the ship or doing other chores – the crew was being paid so they had to earn their pay! Turnaround (in harbour) could be as little as twelve hours. Enough time to unload their cargo, bunker (coal), load new cargo and be under way. A quick turnaround meant less harbour dues and more profit for him and the ship's owners. By now his love of the sea had changed to love of the rewards. His ability to cut costs made him popular with the ship owners, so he was never without a vessel to command for the next thirty years.

During his sea-faring life Captain Jones sailed and part-owned several ships. They included at least ten sailing vessels and twenty-two steamships. The list below was compiled from a collection of papers by Margaret Attwood's cousin Brenda Bayliss (née King); included in it is most of the ships he sailed in and it charts his seagoing career from apprentice to master:

To illustrate times taken around the turn of the century for journeys in sailing vessels and steam ships, I have listed a few details extracted from some of my grandfather's discharge papers. They range in time from 28 March 1889 to 9 March 1901:

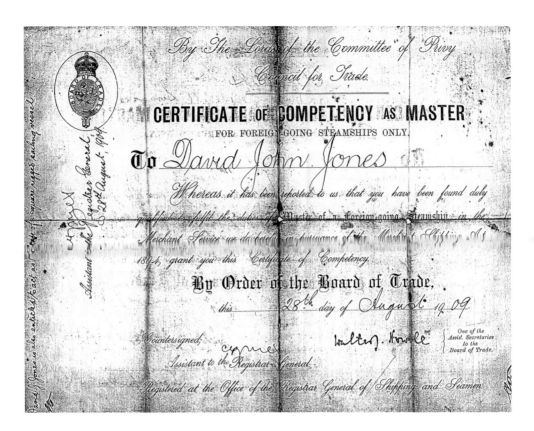

Potato Jones's Master's certificate dated 1909.

Ship's name	Status	Tonnage	Year	Trading
Mary Rose	Apprentice	640	1884	Copper ore
Margaret Ann	Cadet	625	"	"
Carmelita	Able Seaman	558	"	"
Delta	"	537	1889	Coal
Cicero	"	468	1891	
Glanrafon	"	472		
Golconda	"	443		
Hinda	2nd Mate	426		
Andaman	"	756		
Zadok	1st Mate	537		

Ship's name	Status	Tonnage	Year	Trading
Potomac	Able Seaman	198	1890	Sulina, Black Sea
James Drake	"	875	1891	Black Sea
Beaconfield	1st Mate	1,118	1899	Black Sea, Spain
Netherby	"	1,211	1904	Med. Ports
Hatfield	"	1,085	1905	"
Dunsley	2nd Mate	1,254	1906	"
Segontian	1st Mate	736	"	Italy & Spain
Cangarian	"	"	1907	1907
Cardiffian	"	609	1908	1908
Eros	"	1,203	"	"
Demetian	"	695	"	Black Sea, Spain
Cymrian	Master	unknown	1910	Med & Baltic
Segontian	"	"	unknown	Various ports
Menevian	"	"	"	Italy & Spain
Margretian	"	"	"	Baltic & Spain
Penthames	"	"	"	Baltic & Genoa
Bramwell	"	"	1935	Italy & Spain
Bramhill	"	"	1936	Spain
Kellwyn	"	"	1937–39	"

Vessel	Tonnage	Type	hp	Engaged	Destination	Discharged	Months
Carmelita	588	Sail	0	S/sea	Cape Town	Swansea	7
Delta	537	"	"	"	Tucaras	Sharpness	4.5
Potomac	1,198	Steam	150	"	Sulina	Swansea	2
Cicero	468	Sail	0	"	Buenos Aires	"	9.3
James Drake	875	Steam	130	"	Tramping	"	4
Glanrafon	472	Sail	"	"	Pt. Nolloth	"	5.5
Glanrafon	"	"	"	"	Cape Town	"	6.5
Golconda	443	"	"	"	Pt. Nolloth	"	7
Beaconsfield	1,118	Steam	160	Glasgow	Elba	Glasgow	1.5
Beaconsfield	"	"	"	"	Naples	"	"
Beaconsfield	"	"	"	"	Genoa	"	"
Beaconsfield	"	"	"	"	Alexandria	"	2

Margaret Attwell:

It is obvious from journey times taken that steam was overtaking sail. The return journey in sailing ships was anyone's guess. But even in very slow steamships, return journeys to and from Italian ports took a planned six weeks whilst sail was always at the mercy of the fickle winds.

Although a barque could attain speeds of 15 knots in favourable conditions, as opposed to a steam vessels 5 knots, a steam ship could sail directly into the wind and was never becalmed. A square rigger could only sail about 65° to the wind, so it may tack for days to reach its port of destination. Steam ships required a small crew, which helped to balance the cost of coal and maintenance. Steam ships were also made larger so they could carry sufficient tonnage to compensate for space taken by machinery.

This said, it was to be 1888 before the number of steamships entering Swansea harbour exceeded those of sail. In 1888, 2,447 steamships brought in 954,040 tons of registered tonnage against 1,147 sailing vessels which carried a mere 306,255 registered tons. The next year steamships brought in over one million tons of goods while sail managed 296.019 and a terminal decline had set in.

Sail continued until the 1930s. After the Second World War a few French onion ketches sailed into North Dock for a further ten years. Apart from pleasure craft trading by sail ended around 1950.

Captain 'Potato' Jones' nautical career was far from over though. By 1935 he had formed the Dillwyn Steamship Co. and two years later they owned four vessels. It as during the period of the Spanish Civil War in the late 1930s that he earned the sobriquet 'Potato' for allegedly running guns during the blockade of Spain. From his own records we know that 'Potato Jones' was trading with Spain between 1935-39 and as there was little money to be made delivering potatoes to Spain at this time, it is entirely conceivable he was trading guns. Guns in – refugees out goes the family legend and Captain 'Potato' Jones became a legend for his many hair-raising exploits avoiding the Spanish, German and British navies. He retired in 1940 and died in 1962 at the ripe old age of ninety-two.

There is no documentary evidence to suggest that Captain Nicholas ever met Captain Jones, although both started out from Swansea. This is not too surprising as the former was twenty-seven years older than the latter and his career as a master came to an end in 1909 just as Captain Jones's was starting. By comparison with 'Potato Jones', Captain Nicholas has left less detail about which ships he crewed beyond what he mentions in his diaries. It is not unthinkable that they knew of one another and crossed each others path in late nineteenth-century Swansea.

four

Harry and Benjamin Davies – Upper Bank Coppermen

If the diaries of two Swansea sea captains have aroused your interest then the next chapter should sustain it. I got the idea for it after seeing an old family photograph belonging to Mr and Mrs John and Joan Roach. It showed a group of workers from the Upper Bank Copper Works. The photograph was taken at some point around 1902-05 and contained a man called Henry (Harry) Davies who lived his life between 1873-1946. An initial interest in what I thought was the life of an ordinary working man in late-Victorian Swansea took me on an interesting voyage of discovery. It also taught me a lesson in making assumptions about the sort of life that people led in towns like Swansea and the life opportunities they offered.

The 1901 Census described Harry's occupation as 'furnaceman' and he lived with his wife Elizabeth Anne in Grenfell Town on the east side of Swansea. According to experts at the National Museums & Galleries of Wales that I have consulted, Harry was a 'rollerman'; we can tell this because of the distinctive tongs he is holding in the photograph. It is likely that he was involved in sending bars of copper through steam-driven rollers and converting them into copper sheet. Such sheet went all over the world even as far afield as India. Photographs exist in the City & County Museum Collection of Swansea Museum which shows teams of men (albeit in the Hafod Works in the 1920s) at work on the rollers. Diminutive men in caps and aprons wield large tongs which are feeding copper sheet into machinery that dwarfs them. If we assume the date of Harry's photograph to be around 1901, then the Upper Bank Works was already in the combined ownership of Williams Foster and Pascoe Grenfell & Co. Ltd, who between them owned the works between 1892-1924. This came about because in 1892 the Grenfell family put the Middle and Upper Bank Copper Works into voluntary liquidation. They did this because family interest in the firm had been on the wane since 1879 when Pascoe St Leger Grenfell died. After his death a succession of much younger male members of the family and works managers, apparently chosen for their religious piety rather than business sense, took over. The end came quite suddenly with an abrupt announcement in *The Cambrian* newspaper of 21 October 1892 that the Grenfell's were retiring from the family business. The company had obviously been ailing because Harry and his workmates had taken two wage cuts of 5 per cent before the closure was announced. Unions were in existence by then and we know that Harry was a keen union man. However, active militancy tended to be curtailed by supposedly 'older and wiser' members of the workforce whose tendency it was to be deferential to the 'masters'. So much so that in August 1850 there was even a cricket match played between 'men and masters' and played in the best of spirit too. A team made up of Kilvey copperworkers played a one-day game against a team led by Starling Benson (1808-1879). He was the owner of the nearby Forest Copperworks, chairman of the Harbour Trust and chairman of Swansea Vale Railway. The Kilvey men won by an innings and thirty-eight runs. That the Grenfell's own brand of benevolent paternalism worked to keep the workforce largely docile is proved by the fact that between 1844 and 1879 there was not a single strike when the works was managed by Pascoe St Leger Grenfell. That the Grenfell's were known to charge rents at least 25 per cent higher than the Vivians charged their workers at the White Rock Works seems not to have been held against them. Twenty-six years before Harry was born in 1847, the Grenfell's charged 6d a room as rent and when all the houses at Pentrechwyth were offered for sale in the 1892 liquidation sale, they were valued at under £100. Still, the news that Upper Bank was closing, which by then had been in Grenfell's hands since 1804, would have fallen like a bombshell on Harry and his workmates. The capital value of Upper Bank and its machinery had been calculated at £150,000-£200,000, while it was still a business. In liquidation and as scrap, the sum total of the individual parts was reckoned at a mere £40,000. Fortunately the Cornish firm of Williams Foster & Co. of Morfa took over and Upper Bank and became Williams, Foster & Pascoe Grenfell. The Grenfell's retained a single seat on the board. This in sharp contrast to when the family firm became a limited company in 1890, when all the shares were bought by the Grenfell's and all their relatives.

Harry retired early, so the family has it, due to ill health brought on by his exposure to copper fumes from the furnaces. Because of a lack of provision for 'early retirement' in those days, he was fortunate to receive a small retainer from the union to carry on as its secretary. John Roach can still remember being ushered into the kitchen out of the way when men came to Harry's house in Grenfelltown to pay their union dues. Harry's grandson Alan Roach told me:

> Harry was a keen student of politics and during the Second World War he had a more or less standing committee of like-minded friends who assisted him at 1 Grenfelltown, Sam and Tommy John were two of whom I remember. They discussed a wide range of issues one I recall was the debate about the second front being demanded by Soviet Russia.

Although Harry was an invalid by this stage of his life he was, says Alan Roach:

> … a much-respected secretary of the local Transport & General Workers Union. The impression one got from the comings and goings of Union members, was that he ran the branch from his large wooden armchair. He was in some ways like a King holding court and therefore rarely on his own at home as his advice was always being sought on industrial relations. In person he was a very calm and kindly man and a very good listener.

Upper Bank, in the form of Williams Foster & Grenfell, carried on until 1924 when it was bought up by British Copper Manufacturers. Upper Bank was the fifth oldest of the Swansea Valley metallurgical concerns after the Llangyfelach Works (1717), the Cambrian Works (1720), White Rock (1737) and Middle Bank (1755). It was started around 1757 by Chauncey Townsend and John Smith. The former was a London merchant and the latter a coal owner from Gwernllwynchwyth. Initially Upper Bank produced lead and spelter (zinc), then copper and lead, then just copper between 1782 and 1828. It diversified into 'yellow metal', which was also known as 'Muntz metal', an alloy composed of 60 per cent copper and 40 per cent zinc. It was used in the sheathing of ship's hulls to protect them from attack by teredo worm or barnacle growth. Copper is ideal in this respect as it is a 'biostatic' metal which means it resists bacterial growth. Then for most of the time between 1850 and 1924 Upper Bank was a copper and spelter works. In a way we just cannot conceive of now, the world was then Swansea's oyster. In the year Harry appears in the group photograph holding his rollerman's tongs, the population of Swansea stood at 94,537. In 1851 it had been 31,139. It had tripled in fifty years. In 1901 1,556 sailing ships imported 192,403 tons of registered tonnage into the port. At the same time 3,413 steam-powered vessels imported 1,757,845 registered tons of goods. The combined tonnage imported by 4,969 vessels (steam and sail) amounted to 1,950,248 tons or nearly 2 million tons of imported goods. The year before, in 1900, some 2.38 million tons of coal left Swansea making it the third largest exporter of coal after Newport (3.98 million tons) and a long way after Cardiff (17.52 million tons). In 1901 the

The headstone of one Robert Davies in the Cemeterio de Ingles at Coquimbo, Chile. There are six Davies buried there including an Elizabeth Davies who died on 2 June 1862. As yet, family history research has not determined whether they were relatives of Harry and Benjamin Davies.

Swansea that Harry Davies lived in traded with the world in a way that seems inconceivable now. Its trading hinterland stretched from Canada to South America, from Scandinavia to the Falkland Islands near Antarctica.

Nearer home, Harry Davies inhabited a paternalistic world where his employer (Pascoe St Leger Grenfell) built his home (Grenfelltown, Rifleman's Row and Taplow Terrace can all still be seen today) the church where he might have worshipped (All Saints Church, Kilvey) and where he may have gone for entertainment (Foxhole Music Hall). Although the latter would not have featured comedy and 'musical turns' as such, it would have most likely been religious instruction in one form or another. In 1851, twenty-two years before Harry was born, a religious Census revealed that the town (as opposed to the suburbs) could on any one Sunday accommodate two-thirds of its 31,000-plus inhabitants in its thirty-one churches and chapels.

In terms of his immediate environment at Pentrechwyth the Grenfell's probably owned every building that Harry encountered, apart from when he went into Swansea town proper.

Harry's father Benjamin Davies was born in 1850 and the Census of 1861 records him as being eleven years of age and at school. By the time of the 1871 Census he was living at 'Grenfell Town, Llansamlet Lower and Glamorgan'. He was living with Rees Walters (aged 53) and his wife Elizabeth (forty-seven), who had two daughters one who was resident and the other living away, but visiting on the day of the Census. The household was a fairly crowded one, as there were seven people in it. In addition to Mr and Mrs Walters and their daughter Mary (nineteen) there were four members of the Davies family living there as stepsons and daughters. How this came about is yet to be discovered. They were Benjamin (twenty-one), Elizabeth (sixteen), Martha (fourteen) and his thirteen-year-old brother Robert. Intriguingly the birthplace of this brother is down as 'Chili' (Chile) at *Guayacán*. The exotic nature of his birthplace is not difficult to understand once you discover that Guayacán was a mining port near the city of Coquimbo in Northern Chile. At the time that Robert somehow came to be born there in 1858, it was the site of the worlds' largest copper mine. Such was the amount of trade between Britain and South America at that time, that in 1865 an English cemetery was established there. Swansea's Capehorner vessels would have been running to and fro all the time and fatalities from yellow fever would have made it a grim necessity. A surviving family relative, Alan Price Roach, thinks Benjamin must have been a 'technical employee' as he can remember his grandfather Harry referring to him 'as a bit of a gaffer'. Family legend has it that Benjamin, in his capacity as 'a technical' made a number of trips to North America and at least one to Pittsburgh in America. In the course of one of these trips he was presented with a decorated walking cane, which still exists and is in the ownership of his great-grandson Peter Davies. By the 1881 Census, when Harry was seven years of age and registered as a 'scholar' (i.e. at school) his father was a rollerman at the copper mill, presumably Upper Bank. Interestingly there is no trace of Benjamin in the 1891 Census or his family. Unfortunately the equivalent Census for America (1890) only exists in fragmentary form and so we cannot confirm that the family is actually there. Family legend has it that the family removed temporarily to America and this was why Harry later came to be known as 'Harry the Yank', although never to his face says his grandson Alan Roach. Interestingly the walking cane bears an inscription that suggests that Benjamin may in some way have been connected to the Ancient Order of Foresters. They were one of the 170 lodges affiliated to various friendly societies that existed in the year of Harry's birth in 1873. Whether they were called 'Oddfellows' or 'Ivorites's' (a specifically Welsh version), they existed to provide sickness or social benefits in the absence of company or state-sponsored equivalents. Quite how Benjamin might have become involved or how this took him (if it did) to America is still to be discovered. The family surface again in the 1901 Census and were living at No. 120 Pentrechwyth Road, Swansea. Benjamin was fifty-one years of age by then and a rollerman still, while Harry (by then twenty-seven years of age) was down as a 'crane driver copper works'. Harry married Elizabeth Anne Thomas on September 19 of that year. On the marriage certificate his 'rank or profession' was recorded as a 'hydraulic crane man at the docks'. He lived at No. 120 Colorado Terrace at Pentrechwyth and his wife lived at No. 4 Gwyndy Terrace in the same parish. Harry was to raise five children, Elizabeth Novello (1902-85), Gwen (1905-90), Harry (1908-2004), Hubert (1915-92) and Benjamin (1917-63). There are three surviving photographs of Harry that poignantly capture him at various stages in his life. The first comes from around 1905 and shows him as a rollerman at the Upper Bank Copperworks. He is probably about thirty-two years of age and looks young and vigorous. The next photograph shows him in 1928 in middle age. The illness that was to curtail his working life seems to be taking effect and he looks thin and gaunt. The photograph was taken at a relative's house in Solva where he went to recuperate. The final photograph shows him in old age in 1944 when he was seventy-one. He looks unwell and broken by ill-health, his chest problems exacerbated possibly by the bowel cancer that would kill him two years later. He was sitting on the window cill of No. 1 Grenfelltown in Pentrechwyth when this photograph was taken, this house can still be seen. Fresh water would have been drawn from a well the Grenfell's had drilled at the north-eastern corner of the terrace or from a leat (a man-made watercourse) leading from the east side of Kilvey Hill to the Vivian's White Rock Copperworks. The stonework of Harry's house is almost certainly Pennant sandstone from a local quarry with probably blocks of copper slag used on the quoins (corners). You can also still see these used as kerbstones to some of the houses. Harry's son Henry J. Davies was present when he died on 26 July 1946. Harry's life, speculative visit to America in the 1890s notwithstanding, would have been lived out mainly within the confines of Pentrechwyth. A working life of six days a week and twelve-hour shifts at Upper Bank would have left him with precious little leisure time he could actually use. A plain and inexpensive headstone in a cemetery in Llansamlet is all that remains of Harry's life, outside family mementoes and faded photographs.

Amazingly, a diary belonging to Harry's father Benjamin has survived and although in a precarious condition, has been transcribed on the following pages. Benjamin was a passenger on a vessel, conceivably a Capehorner, plying the copper trade between Swansea and Chile. As yet family history research does not tell us what the name of the ship was or which year it sailed in. Although there is a suggestion that it might have been sometime between 1872 and 1879 to judge by the date on which Christmas Day falls in the log. He does not appear from the diary to have functioned as a crew member so one must assume he was going out to South America as a 'technical' expert. Little is known on what terms these men would have gone out on, whether they were allowed to take families and such like. The diary is transcribed below. I have tried wherever possible to keep to the spelling and punctuation that Benjamin used as this keeps the flavour of his journal intact. Nevertheless I have had to intercede at some points because of some undecipherable wording or a word which was mis-spelt out of all recognition:

… Wednesday 15th day [out] all well fair wind going 7 knots. This day we had gin sould by auction. Morgan sold half pint gin for one shilling to David Thomas, William John, Thomas Richards and John Norris which concluded all the liqueurs they had. So everyone have to drink Adam's Ale [presumably water] for the future.

Friday 17th Day. Clear and calm going three knots at 8:o'clock and Nadera (Madeira?) stood 61 miles distance East and South. The weather is getting verrey hot. We are all lying about our wives and children poor Morgan is verrey often wishing he had the small gang with [him] and we are verrey often plaguing him about it …

Saturday 18th day [out?] Clear morning vessel going 3 knots with a fair wind and all her sail spread and that is a splendid view to see a vessel in full sail. 8 o'clock read Luke Chap. 10.

Sunday 19th Day. Clear and calm with not a breath of wind, the vessel is drifting about. We enjoyed the Sabbath verrey well we spent it reading and singing. We had a long talk with the second mate about marriage and divorcement [divorce?] as you know it is natural for sailors to talk about women,

Harry Davies is second from the right kneeling in this works photograph taken at the Upper Bank Copperworks around 1901.

when they have got a leisure hour. So he lead us past scripture but Chap. 24. 12345. So we varied in opinions and we led him back to the New Testament …

Thursday 23rd day. Clear morning N.E. brees going 6½ knots. At 6 o'clock am we were called out of bed by the Captain to see one of old Jonathan large ships close under out lee side called the Andalsea of Ballemarie [?] directly afterwards we were called up to see the flying fish for the first time we even saw them. So we had the pleasing view of seeing them flying from 20 to 60 yeards and some a 100 yeards before they droped. At 10 o'clock am we imployed ourselves in getting our beds on deck to give them air for first time since we left Swansea. 8 o'clock pm read Acts. Chap. 5 …

Saturday 25th day. Clear morning soft brees going 6 knots. This morning at 2 o'clock we crossed the tropic of Cancer lat. 23½° N Long. 23° 48 W. The American ship is still within two or three miles of us and flying fish in swarms all around us. We have been talking a great deal about our wives and Swansea market, one saying he could see his wife in such a place bying such a thing and another saying he could see his on somewhere else etc. This is all we got to do sometimes reading and sometimes singing and leying about the decks in all figures and forms …

Sunday 26th day. Clear morning steady brees going 7 knots. This day we imployed ourselves in reading and singing at 10 o'clock an English man of war steamer bore down towards us with her St. George's pennant flying wanting to know who we were and what we were. So we answered and told her. But to tell you the hole of, as she was coming towards us the sun glittered on her bright

Harry Davies in middle age at some point in the 1930s when staying at a relative's house at Solva.

Harry Davies in old age shortly before his death and when he was living at No. 1 Grenfelltown, Pentrechwyth.

The very modest gravestone of Harry Davies.

brasswork so that a person might have thought that she was firing of guns at us. So Morgan was forward in the bow so he ran back and told the captain that she had fired two guns at us. Laughter through the ship. 8 o'clock read St. James Chap. 3 …

Tuesday 28 day. Clear all is well stiff brees going 8 knots, at 9 o'clock am we were in site of another of Cape Verde islands. Which is called Brava and we had a splendid view of it. It looked verrey rockey and some verrey high cliffs appearing very much like the [undecipherable] of [undecipherable] at 10 o'clock am we were in site of another called Togo / Fogo this one have verrey high peackes in it estimated at 9,700 feet above the level of the water. 11 o'clock came on a calm so we had to drift

Detail showing the end of Benjamin Davies's walking cane with inscription.

about. 2 o'clock the cook gave one of the little pigs a blow in the head and killed him. So we bled him and cleaned and dressed him. At 3 o'clock pm thear came a shark alongside. So we went out with the lock [flintlock rifle?] and a pice of pork on it and caught him and bought him on board and killed him. He was 6 feet long he had one young one in his belly. We had a piece of the old one to tea and it eat verrey well. Verrey much like veal.

Wednesday 29th day. Clear and calm. The vessel is to a stand. Today at noon we had half the pig to dinner and we ate it all. Wm. John and myself had the head to ourselves and two ribs each. So I can ashore you between a good apetite and a nice piece of pork we made a good dinner. We injoyed our dinner so well that it almost tempted us for him to give the other a blow tomorrow. 8 o'clock read Cor [Corinthians] Chap. 13.

Thursday 30th day. Clear and calm at 7 o'clock am a lot of black fish came close to the ship from 15 to 20 of them and we had a fine view they are the next in size to the whale [dolphins?]. At 8 am there came a strong brees and we …

Friday 31st day, clear morning and all is well a good brees from the East and be South vessel going 7 knots 5 o'clock pm we passengers and the Captain we are all sitting down on the bows verrey comfortable talking about one thing and the other and vessel going 7 knots as before mentioned. In the meantime thear were a dark cloud in the east and with that it began to rain and blow tremendously and struck our sails back against the mast and like that she remained for a few minits and the rain falling as if it came out of buckets. We thought it was all over right us. But it was providence that protected us or else the mastes would have went over board. But she had good way on her and so the helm had her back on corce and so nothing acured only fritened a little 8 o'clock read [undecipherable]. Chap. 2nd.

A tintype image of Benjamin Davies in the possession of the family.

A tintype image of Benjamin Davies's wife, Elizabeth.

Heb Chap first. Saturday 18th day ch
Morning vessel going 3 knots with
a fair wind and all her sail spread
and that is a splendid vew to see a
vessel in ful sail. 8 oclock read Lu
Chap 16th. Sunday 19 day clear and
calm not a breath of wind the vessel
is drifting nows we enjoyed the sab
verrey well we spent it reading an
singing. We had a long talk with
the second mate about marrage and
devorcement as you know it is natu
ral for sailors to talke about women
when they have got a leasure hour.
So he led us to part Scripture Det Cha
24. 1 2 3 4 5. So we carried on conver
sions. and we led him back to the
new testament Mat Chap 5. ver.
31 32. Chap 19. 1 2 3 4 5 6 7 8 9. Mar
Chap 16. 2 &c. 8 oclock read 1st Joh
Chap 20. Monday 20 day clear
morning soft breez going 4 kno
nothing particular to day. 8 oclo
read Luke Chap 7. Tuesday 21 da

A page from a notebook or log kept by Benjamin Davies whilst travelling from Swansea to Chile by boat in the 1870s.

Since we left Swansea 8 oclock
P M read Act Chap 5. Friday 24
day Clear morning and all is well
We are now in the North East trade
and a good breez going 7 knots. 8
oclock read 1th Tim Chap 4. Satura
25 day Clear morning soft breez
going 6 knots. This morning
at 2 oclock We Crossed the tropice
of Cancer Lat 23½ N long 25 &
West. the American Ship is still
Within two or three miles of us
and fleying fish in swarms all
around us. We have been talking
a great deal about our Wives an
Swansea market. one saying
he Could see his [Wife] in such a place
byeing such a thing and another
saying he Could see his in some
whare else &c. This is all We go
to do some times reading and som
times singing and saying about
the dishes in all figures and form

A second page from the log of Benjamin Davies, a rare surviving document written by a
Swansea copperman of that period.

Saturday November the 1st day. Cloudy morning and verrey squaly and verrey heavey rain and a vessel in site but she stood to far off to know who she was. 8 o'clock read Nat. Chap. 27.

Sunday 2nd day. Cloudy steady brees 7 knots. Until about 10 o'clockm am it blackened all around and it began to blow and rain and we had much sail on her. When it began that the vessel we are berring herself before we could shorten the sail. First of all gose her flying gib then her fore top gallant sail and the gib by this time we really thought her mastes weare going and it had not been a good one and good gearing away they would have went. This weare the time that Ingland expected every man to do his duty such times as this would make every eye witness wonder how poor sailers doth spend thear mony so foolish. So in about a hour we got under close reef top sails and we weare all quite comfortable at 8 o'clock pm read 1st [undecipherable] Chap. 1st.

Monday 3rd day. Clear and calm at 11 o'clock am thear came a large shark alongside of us. But before we could get the hook ready he was away he was about ten feet long. 8 o'clock read John Chap 1st.

Thursday 4 day. Cloudy and squally vessel going 7 knots 2 o'clock pm our carpenter speared a verrey nice fish about 5 lbs. weight called the Bereta or the SkipJack [Tuna]. We are now in lat 6° North long 23 West. 8 o'clock read Rom [Romans] Chap 2.

Wensday 5 day clear morning going 8 knots we are now in the South East trades about 4 degrees North of the line or Equator. On the 17th of last month a full riged [rigged] ship under American coolers sliped on ahead of us and soon got out of site. So yesterday we came with again and now we are along side of her and both carring as much canvas as they can according to wind and weather. 8 o'clock read Chap John Chapt 15.

Thursday 6 day. Clear morning going 9 knots the American vessel right apasite [opposite] us about 2 miles distance. Both running close to the wind. Carring every stick of canvas as they an put on according to wind and corce. 8 o'clock read Ephes [Ephesians] Chap 3.

Friday 7 day. Clear morning and in good health and a good brees going 8 knots. This morning we crossed the great line that is so often talked about at home and abord ship in long 26° West. So now we are expecting old neptewn abord every minit to share all his young children that never were across the line before. But wheather he will come or not I will let you know some future time, the American vessel is still along side of us but to witch of our lots it will fall to be behind at least I don't know. At 8 o'clock pm we were under the senter of the moon, read Act Chap 19.

Saturday 8 day. Clear morning and all in good health. Stif brees going 7 knots. We have lost site of the American ship. We exspect she is gone away to windward [that is to the east] 8 o'clock read gal [?] Chap 2.

Sunday 9 day. Clear weather making 7 knots. We spent this partly in reading and singing. About 5 o'clock pm the passengers and the captain talking about something or another but what ever. Wm John's bitch went on to the galley and one of the sailors throughed hot coffee all over her. So the poor bitch came back screeching back to tell in a most dredful maner. Witch disturbed our minds verrey much. 8 o'clock read Act Chap 26.

Monday 10th day clear nothing to be seen but the blue sky on the wite wild ocean. This day we had the water served out to us for the first time. By the captains orders. 3 quarts a day. Each man and also we had rice instead of peas at our own request. Read 2 Cor [Corinthians] Chap 5.

Wensday 12th day clear and clam vessel drifting about 1 knots. Now I am going to tell you how we are getting on with the vittles. The beef and pork and peas. It is a nough [enough] to say that we cant eat it and a nother thing to say we can't aford water a nough to boil rice out of three quarts per day. We could make a cup of tea or coffee if we had water. So now you can see it bad to be on the regular lowance of water in warm climates but a passenger will do verrey well with it in cold climates. 8 o'clock pm read [undecipherable] Chap 9.

Wensday 14 day clear and a soft brees going 3 knots. The same fare as yesterday 4 pm some vessels homewards bound but all of them to far to speak to them. 8 o'clock read Ephes. Chap. 1st at 10 pm thear came a Barck [Barque?] under our lee bows bound to Bristol called the Elgen and we told her to report us in the Gazetta when she got home and she promised to do so. 8 o'clock read 1 Cor. Chap. 15.

Saturday 15' day clear morning all well a soft brees going 3 knots. This day we had potatoes and salt cod fish for dinner wich the Captain Charaty [charitably] bestowed upon us and that aloud with a little vinegar and mustard we made a good dinner. 8 pm read Ephes. Chap 3.

Sunday 16th day. Clouday morning strong brees from the N.E the vessel stearing South west making 9 knots we spent the day partly in reading and singing 8 pm read Rom Chap 12th.

Monday 17th day. Cloudy morning at 5 o'clock am it came on to rain tremendously and it rained all day and made some of the heaviest showers I ever seen with my eyes. At 8 o'clock am the wind shifted to the South and we stearing SW by South. So we had a headwind and a cross sea. So I can asure you we had a verrey ruff day of it and not that alone but we had a awfull fight between the second mate and a little yankey they abused each other verrey much and we were verrey much afraid that it would have rose to a mutany [mutiny] abord the ship but they were sepearted thanks be to the Lord for it and the captain gave orders that the first man that would rise his hand should be put in irons emeditaely [immediately]. So it is all peassable [peaceable] thanks be to the Lord for it and we are quite comfortable. 8 o'clock read Rom 14 Chap.

Tuesday 18th day. Clear morning and the vessel going 4 knots. This day I employed myself mending Morgans old trousers. So today I began my tailoring but when I shall end it I don't know. What ever I sopose if I live I shall have to carre it on for another five years at the least. 8 o'clock read Rom Chap 13th.

Wensday 19 day. Clear and calm vessel making 1 knots. We are all injoying good health and I am to tell that my chest is much better that what I have felt this last few years and if I live to see my jurney end I hope it will be quite well. 8 pm read James Chap 2.

Friday 21 day clear an all is well. Soft brees fair wind going 5 knots. Some homewards bounder in site but verrey far off. 8 pm read Luke Chap 13th.

Saturday 22 day. Clear and all is well soft brees going 3 knots. We eat fish on everrey Saturday to distinguish ourselves from the Roman Catholics because they eat the fish on Friday. This evening we had another row abord ship. The cause of it was the steward got drunk and failed to carry the tea aft for he was too drunk to carry himself … and as he came on the quarter deck the Captain noticed [him] coming along staggering and followed him down to the cabin and acuesed him of been drunk. So you might easy know what was the answer. because a drunken man always says he is sober … and at the same time could scarsly say bread [author's note: you can still hear this expression in use in Swansea today]. So now the steward is back in the cabin again. And the Captain takes good care of the keys … but he has lost his carictor [character]. So my conclusion is this … that temperance is [as] good on sea as well as on land. So my dear wife and friends and neybours I hope you will take an advice from a poor unworthy that it is to refrain from all intoeseating [intoxicating] liquors and hold stedfast to temperance because drunkards shall never inherit the Kingdom of Heaven 1 Cor. 6 read 8 o'clock pm St. James Chap 4. Sunday 23th day. Clear morning good brees going 7 knots. This day we imployed ourselves as usual in reading and singing at 12 o'clock for dinner nothing but a bit of boiled cow because as before mentioned we could not eat the beef or pork and we had eat all our preserved meat through the week. 3 o'clock pm thear appeared three large fish in site wich is called Black fish. As before mentioned on the 30th day of Oct last but theas wear much larger. Theas wear about 20 to 25 feet long and great breath in them as well [whales?]. It was wonderfull to see theair great carcasis many yards out of the water to any person that had never seen only the little native fishes of the rivers of Wales at 8pm read Rom 2 Chap …

Monday 24 day fair and a roff [rough] sea going 8 knots at 8 o'clock read 1 Cor Chap 6 pm going 16 knots.

Tuesday 25th day. Cloudy morning 6 o'clock strong brees going 8 knots, 11 o'clock am it came on to blow a gale of wind and remaine blowing harder and harder until at last we could scarsly show our canvas and at 1 o'clock we war forst to heave to under a close reef main top sail and a small gib. So all the sail we had was not much larger than two good blankets and it continued until about twelve o'clock that night and then it abated. But the sea running mountains high. We are now in Lat 34° 30 South Long 41° 33 West this is nearly off the river de la Plata, or as the sailors call it the river Plate. I have mentioned before about some squalls and about it blowing. But what was it to this. It blew so hard in this gale that we could not steady ourselves on the deck for the wind or scarsly walk at all. This is the first time we failed to read and pray in public because the vessel was rolling so much we could not stand on our feet. But I belive that wear some secret prayers sent up. This morning Morgan catched a patigonia ship on top of the house on deck. William John said it was a verrey rare thing to see a duck catching a snip [snipe?] I shot two Cape hens but they fell into the sea. Read St. John Chap 9.

Wensday 26th day. Clear morning but the sea is running verrey high after the gale yesterday but she held her own. We are now in Lat 35° 3' South Long 48° 42' West. This day we saw several whales blowing and spouting the water up into the air. But they were to far for us to see the fish itself. 8 o'clock read Cor Chap6.

Thursday 27 day clear morning and clam not a breath of wind the vessel is all to a stand and lots of cape hens and pidgeons and other little birds all around the ship. S the Captain found powder and shot and we found guns and there was a regular shuting match. Pleas not to tell John Bull or else perapts he will fine us for shuting the game on the great Atlantic park. 6 o'clock pm thear came on a soft brees and increased until 8 pm and then we wear going 9 knots and a strong brees all night. 8 o'clock read [?] Chap 2nd.

Friday 28 day a verrey wild morning at 9 o'clock the wind shifted to the South west and our corce wear S.W. half south. So you can see we had a head wind and at the same time it came on to blow a gale of wind and lasted 10 hours and by that [time] the sea weare running mountains high. And everrey whare threatening to sweep our decks. But thanks be to the lord and to him alone for it was through his kind providence that preserved us. 8 pm read Cor Ch 4.

Saturday 29 day clear morning but a verrey ruff sea after the gale and the wind blowing from the south, o we could not make scarsly any way at all. 8 o'clock pm read John Chap 15

Sunday 30 day clear and calm scarsly a breath of wind. We spent this day as usial in reading and singing 6 o'clock pm thear came about 8 or 9 whales all around blowing in all directions thear came three close to us verrey near as large as the ship herself. Read 2nd [undecipherable] Chap 3.

Monday December the first day. Cloudy morning fine brees from the N E going 8 knots 10 o'clock am we wear going 10 knots to 10½ knots at 6 o'clock pm we had to reef top sails 8 o'clock read 2 [undecipherable] Chap 3.

Tuesday 2 day. Clear morning head wind soft brees stearing five points of our corse going 3 knots. 8 pm read [undecipherable] Chap 3. at 11 o'clock came on to blow a gale of wind from the SW and lasted until morning six o'clock.

Wensday 3 day clear sky but the sea looking verrey wild and rolling verrey heavy 8 'o'clock thear came a verrey large whale along side the largest our Captain ever seen. She kept company with us for many hours sometimes one side and sometimes the other side of the ship. In the afternoon we saw a verrey large shark under out stern fast asleep. 8 o'clock read John Chap 6.

Thursday 4 day clear cold morning fair wind going 6 knots stearing S.W. half South at 11 o'clock and it came on to blow from the S.W and it blowed that hard that we could scarsly show any canvas at all, and lasted for 36 hours at 2 o'clock the whale fish appeared in view again blowing at everrey wave. By seeing these whales often brought me in mind of Jona [Jonah] in the whales belley. So I was looking at the whale and thinking of gods wonderful works in the creation and thinking as well that it could have been done, because he and a few more might a went in easy and lived verrey comfortably. At 8 pm read Heb. [Hebrews] Chap 10th.

Friday 5 day wild morning blowing verrey hard and head wind and verrey cold. We had several showrs of hailstone today. We had only three sails on the ship [undecipherable] and two reef in the main top sail close reef and fore top mast and fore top mast stay sail. 8 pm read [undecipherable] 12.

Saturday 6th day clear morning coming in to a calm at 2 pm we wear in a regular calm again. At 3 pm thear came on a soft brees and increased until 12 o'clock midnight and that time we wear going 9 knots with a heavy sea on again. Then it was all hand on deck again to reef top sails and by this time she had so much pressure on her that was shoving her more through the water to that degree so that she was shiping the water over her bows until she had three feet of water on the deck before we could get the sails in. 8 pm read St. John Chap 19th.

Sunday 7 day fine morning the wind abated again a great deal and we have begun to spread our sails again. We spent our Sunday as usual in reading and singing verrey comfortable sometimes walking about the deck. We had a little conversation about thing that wear [a] rose out of chapter that was read last night. One thing was how long was Jesus Christ in the grave some said it was three days and three nights, and others that he was only two nights and a day between them. This evening it came on to blow again but we wear better prepared for it this evening than we war last night because we had not half the sail on her. At 8 pm read [undecipherable] Chap 12.

Monday 8 day. At 8 am thear came a lot of whales up close to the ship from 10 to 19 of them and we had a splendid view it is still blowing a stif brees the vessel running close to the wind going 4 knots. At 8 pm read St. James Chap 5th

Tuesday 9 day blowing verrey hard all night. The vessel could scarsly make any way at all. This evening we saw one of the penguins or pengwyn see Gehografi [geography] Josia Thomas Jones on the Falkland island southerly wind getting verrey cold hear. You must understand that it is the southerly wind that brings the frost and snow hear. Like the northerly wind at home: at 8 pm read Phi Chap 1st.

Thursday 11 day. Clear this morning the wind shifted. E are now in Lat 50° … 30'South. Long 55° Stearing SSW. If wind and weather permit we intend to share the Falkland island to morrow morning at the most. Easterly one them our vessel is going 8½ knots. At 8 pm read Phil Chap 2nd.

Friday 12 day at 6pm we all got up to see the Falkland island but we did not have so good a view as we thought yesterday we should have had. Because the wind came on to blow last night at 12 o'clock. So we wear forst [forced] to keep away from them about 20 miles distance. It appeared verrey much like the inglish land at home when it is clear. Although it is barran. Some white sandy places represent the fields of corn and hay: also some Black rocks represents the brushwood an the plantations: so that you could really think it weare the Inglish land it self. Thear is plenty of all kinds of birds flying about hear. Such as Albettrusis [Albatrosses], Cape hen, Cape pidjeons and widewakes etc. At 8 pm read 1 Cor [Corinthians] Chap 6:

Saturday 13th day. Clear morning fair wind the stearing S.W half W. at 8 am our carpenter harpooned a porpis and we hoisted him up under. Bowsprit clear out of the water for a bout 4 minits. But before we could get a lin [line] a round him the harpoon came out and down he went again into the water: so we lost him and I can asure you it was a great lost to us: because we would have made many fresh meals of him: and you might believe me fresh meals is verrey rare on board of vessels going around the horn: at 8 pm read Luke Chap. 10th.

Sunday 14th day clear morning and a fine day all day long and a fine day is verrey rare in this part of the world. We spent it as usial in reading and singing but a head wind tacking back and for all day long: at 8pm read the Epistle of [undecipherable].

Monday 15th day clear morning but verrey cold and still a head wind at 5pm we past a vessel homewards bound. We should have spook to her but it came on to snow and got verrey thick weather. At 8 pm read Luke Chap. 14th.

Tuesday 16th day clear morning today at 10 am the Staten Island appeared in view rite a head of us and whales to be seen close under our lee side. At 6pm we ware within a few miles of it and we had a splended view of the peaks splitting the clouds. Theare are a long ridge of nearly bare rockes with a great many sharper peakes wich the clouds partly covers. That is a fact than many wont belive: I was eye witness seeing the clouds cover some of them and others the cloud would only cover the middle of the peak: so that the bottom and the top would be clear. So you should inderstand that we should see the bottom and the top of the peak at the same time an the middle covered with cloud. We are now in Lat 54° 44' South – Long 63° 29' West. We are now [in] verrey cold weather last night Wm John Morris and myself were obliged to take our dogs to bed with us owing to the cold. So we had comfortable bedfellows for the first time since we left home. At 8pm read St. John Chap. 20th.

Wensday 17th day. Cloudy morning head wind stearing south against our will at 8pm thear came a squall and carried away our flying jib boom and it remained blowing hard all day long. 8pm read 2 [undecipherable] Chap. 3.

Thursday 18 day. Cloudy and squally blowing hard all day and a head wind. Doing no good only going a little to the south against our will it remains verrey cold. At 8pm read Heb. Chap 8.

Friday 19th day. Cloudy the wind is abated but still a head of us. Whale fishes. About us today again. At 8pm read Act. Chap 20.

Saturday 20th day. Clear morning but verrey cold wind still and a head wind. We hove our ship a bout today on the other tack but still going the wrong way. At 8pm read Acts 26. Chap.

Sunday 21 day. Clear and cold and a head wind at 12 midday we had a fair wind. We are now in Lat 57° 55' South Long 66° 51' West. That's nearly right off the Horn. Now we are stearing WSW going 5 knots whale fishes blowing all around us. At 8pm read Acts. Chap.4.

Monday 22 day thick and foggy fair wind stearing WSW making 7 knots. 8 pm read Acts. 27.

Tuesday 23rd day clear morning and calm vessel scarsly moving anyway at all. Today we caught a large Albertrus [Albatross] he measured 10 feet from one point of the wing to the other. His feet measured 8½ inches but at one o'clock pm thear came two bottle nosed whales [dolphins?] and went twice round the ship. At 2 pm the brees freshened up a little and at 4pm it blewed a good brees 5 o'clock thear came another forty whale under our stern and had a regular race [with] us for about forty minits. But he could run closer to the wind that what we could so away she went to windward and we lost site of her at 8pm read Acts. Chap. 25.

Wensday 24 day. Cloudy morning and verrey thick dew in with the wind from the SW blowing us verrey near the land so the orders was gave to … but no land could be seen for the thick weather until 4 o'clock pm when we made it out close to us on our starboard side. The first land we saw was some small islands and then the mainland a short distance the inside of it. It was part of the land of Terra de Fugo [Tierra del Fuego]. So we put the ship about and made out to the SE it was blowing and remained so all night. 8 o'clock read 2 Cor. Chap 13th

Thursday 25th day. Christmas Day and we had a pleasant one. Blowing a gale of wind rold and tossed about. With the sea running mountains high and I hope that you injoyed your Christmas dinner so well as we did. But it is a question wheather you had such a good one as we or not. Because everrey man on board had something extra but we passengers. The sailors had [undecipherable], cabin plum pudding and we had duf and nothing. 8 pm read Acts Chap. 27.

Friday 26th/Saturday 27. Blowing a gale of wind until Sunday morning 28 day it abated at 6 o'clock am. We spread a little canvas again until 6 pm we had to draw it down again so it remained blowing until …

Friday 30th day at 2 o'clock am. We spread our canvas again once more in fair wind, 5 am going 9 knots. 8 pm read Luke 1st Chap.

Wensday 31 day cloudy morning and a head wind stearing S.W. by South. Today at 10am we spook [spoke to] a vessel homewards bound called the Pizzaro of Liverpool. Bound to Swansea she had passengers on board two of them weare Miss Alison our Master's wife and Miss Ross the Inglish Counsel: she promised to gazet us [this means to report they had see them when they reached port]. We met her in Lat 54° 30' South – Long 79° 14' West. Read St. John Chap 8.

Thursday 1st day of January new year's day and might we all as a family serve god more diligently this year that what we did last because it is the [undecipherable] is the only comfort in the time of need. 8 pm read Luke Chap 11th.

Friday 2 day clear morning good brees going towards Chile at the rate of 8 knots. This morning we past another under a lee we spak (spoke] to her. But it was blowing so hard and the two vessels were going so fast so we don't know wheather they understood us or not. We are today in Lat 52° 22' South – Long 81° 15' West. 8 pm read [undecipherable] Chap 4.

Saturday 3 day cloudy and stormy morning going 5 knots we are now aneous [anxious?] to be in Chile to see what is thear and another thing it is 89 days this morning since we left the Mumble head. And it is to long time to be mucking about on the wild ocean, but the worst of it is we don't know how long time we shall be again before we reach out journey end if God doth spare our lives and health. But we ought to be verrey thankfull to him for sparing our lives and for the wondefull good helth we have injoyed since we left Swansea because we never injoyed better in our [lives?] …

There the transcript ends. I am not sure what I find most poignant about this extract. Whether it is the fact he rejoices in the best health he has ever had obtained perhaps because he was away from his heavily polluted home town of Swansea? Or is it the regular Christian worship that he and his fellow passengers find solace in as a respite from the hardships of the voyage. The fact that he does not know long he will be away from his family and whether he will actually survive only adds to its poignancy. Employees in this period were largely powerless by modern standards and as a consequence could be sent hither and thither at the company's bidding. It could even involve being sent to the other side of the world, something for which they were completely unprepared.

I mean that not only in the psychological sense but physically too as they would almost certainly not have been innoculated against yellow fever, typhoid or anything else. Men like Benjamin would have lived lives of regimented routine structured around work with such 'leisure time' as was available centred around simply recovering from work. Imagine how Benjamin must have coped with having time free from work on the voyage, catching and eating fish and generally experiencing the vagaries of the weather. His life would have been turned topsy-turvey. From the man-made world of Upper Bank Copperworks where everything was geared to industry to the watery wastes of the South Atlantic, I wonder how he coped with all the enforced leisure time? With his bible I expect. You have to wonder whether such an experience would have changed him and, if it did, how. It is difficult to think of an equivalent experience today that one could go through that would be so potentially life-changing except space travel to another planet.

The first men to land on the moon were all changed [for better and worse] by their experience, I wonder if Benjamin was. Seeing whales, dolphins and flying fish must have been so amazing to a man who would have had no preparation for seeing them via education. Imagine being a copper worker in Swansea in the 1870s with your whole existence geared to work and then setting out on a voyage that would last the best part of three whole months. A voyage that would put your very existence at the mercy of prevailing weather conditions and without prospect of rescue should anything go wrong. A voyage that would show you all manner of exotic wildlife before dropping you in a foreign country where you would be expected to ply your trade with no date set for your return. A trade that would itself probably put you in the way of danger and disease due to primitive living conditions and with little or no prospect of compensation should you get injured or even die. This was Harry and Benjamin's world. The Victorian world-view saw the planet as just one big basket of resources to be exploited and profited from. People included. This was nowhere more so than in Swansea, where the copper masters used coal to fuel the furnaces and copper ore to produce the finished goods. They also manufactured zinc, lead and even perfected a way of producing sulphuric acid from copper smoke so that little was wasted. Maps of Swansea in virtually any period from the 1840s onwards show the landscape pock marked with quarries and small mine shafts sunk wherever coal seams ran near the surface and there was money to be made. Building stone, gravel pits and trees were all harvested for their commercial value. There was a kind of industrial alchemy at work which turned copper ore into a marketable semi-finished good; copper sheet, tube or wire. Water power was used to power some works initially but even that was tamed as steam power soon took over and water merely became something to confine to strategically placed conduits called canals. Only at sea did the copper masters' yield second best and even then they built docks so that the tide couldn't completely dictate to them when they could load and unload their ships. Further research by the descendants of Benjamin Davies may reveal more about his life in due course.

Benjamin Davies died on 29 October 1912 and was buried in Llansamlet graveyard.

I am led to believe that it was by no mean unusual for key workers at the various copperworks to keep a log of their activities. I suspect such an activity would have been encouraged by an employer eager to keep a record of what was done, when and how much it cost etc. An example of this came down to me very recently via Dr Gwyn Davies of Killay, a retired physicist who very kindly let me see a notebook kept by his maternal grandfather David John (1867-1936) who worked at the Hafod copperworks. According to the 1901 Census he was described as being a 'stone mason'. He was a Morriston man and one of ten children:

The gravestone of Benjamin Davies, still to be found in a graveyard in Llansamlet.

seven boys and three girls. His father, Edward, was a collier born in Llangyfelach. One of David's brothers, Llewellyn John, became the headmaster of Dynevor School in the 1930s. The latter had four children: Dr Davies' mother and three sons, one of whom Bryn became headmaster of Gors School. In the 1881 Census David is listed as aged fifteen and already 'working at Tin House', by the 1891 Census it was 'mason' and by 1901 it was 'stone mason'.

In the Hafod, David John's job seems to have kept him busy repairing all manner of things ranging from furnace linings to toilets. Interestingly he kept a record of not only the jobs he was required to do but also personal matters, including the deaths of fellow workers, friends and family, all of which are dutifully recorded. He recorded matters of national importance too, including a visit by Lloyd George to Morriston in 1916 in the middle of the First World War. Interestingly, he also kept a kind of works' history and recorded the sequence of works' managers and the dates different parts of that vast industrial complex became active or fell out of use. This kind of record, kept by a man who actually worked there, is hugely interesting, all the more so because it was written in his own hand in a notebook that probably lived in an inside coat pocket for a significant part of his working life. The notebook that Dr Davies still has only dates from 1916 until his grandfather retired in 1931, when he was presented with a clock by 'Fellow Workers of BCM' (British Copper Makers). Because of the wealth of personal and day to day material it contains it is more akin to a journal than a log book. Who knows how many other notebooks of this kind were kept by the thousands of men who worked at the Hafod Copperworks between 1810 and 1924? The vast majority of which were probably thrown away or destroyed when the owner either retired or died. I have included a few pages in this book to show what such a journal looked like and the information it contained. On a more poignant level one has remember that, apart from family photographs, this was usually the only tangible item such people would have left behind after a long working life, company retirement gifts aside, although it also appears that the company gave away 'product' as giftware because I discovered that some large copper plates made at the Hafod were given as twenty-first birthday and wedding presents. David John married Hannah Michael in 1893, in the 1891 Census she was described as a 'tin worker', as was her older sister Elizabeth. Her father John Michael was described as a 'steel smelter' and her brother Evan a 'zinc spelterman'. All good metallurgical occupations and ones that would have been duplicated in thousands of families all over Swansea in the 1890s. Hannah was given three copper plates: one on her twenty-first birthday and two others as wedding presents. These large copper dishes survive to this day in the ownership of Dr Davies's brother who lives in the USA.

Aside from the documentary details of such working men's lives there is another tantalising glimpse of this world to be found in the writing of Edith Courtney. In a book of reminiscences of her life in Swansea picturesquely called *A Mouse ran up My Nightie* she recalled 'A Visit to Kilvey Hill':

Then she cleared the table, and quickly I was dressed in outdoor clothing, Mother smothering my face with cold cream because of the wind. Father took off his collar and tie and sighed into his deep armchair. His canvassing for the day was over, now it was time for Mother and me to go collecting. We went out and the wind cut us pink. We went down, but turned off, towards the mountain, and I clutched Mother's hand in delight. We were the other side of the shunting yards, and now we were on the bank of the canal, and there, on the rust and silver water, just against the steps, bobbed a little boat.

The lean, leather-skinned man seemed elderly, and saw us coming. He stood up, his hands clutching the stonework beyond out feet, the boat swaying under him. He called, and the wind whipped his voice away. Mother held her full dark skirts about her with one hand and me with the other as we went down the slippery steps.

'You never bin on a ferry afore?' the man said to me, and he didn't have a coat, just a striped flannel; shirt with the sleeves rolled up, and his arms were brown and alive with muscle. I shook my head and the boast surged and dipped as Mother sat. I went carefully beside her, facing the man, and to my delighted horror he began to row. The boat left the wall!

Water bubbled near my feet. 'I must get a plank across there', the man said, and his neck went taut as he pulled the boat on.

From water and the opposite bank my fascinated gaze rose to the stark, hoar-frost-covered, Kilvey Hill before us. All its aspirations to greenery murdered by the works at its feet; copper, spelter, tin, all spouting smoke that was laden with fumes and chemical debris. Pollution as it is never seen today. To me then, and to me today, Kilvey Hill is beautiful. Tricks of the weather bring it closer or move it further away, but that Christmas just after my seventh birthday, Kilvey Hill exuded dominance, power, and I was suitably awed.

The Ferry man mentioned in this extract was almost certainly David John Clarke who operated the White Rock Ferry during the 1920s. The Clarkes were a respected family in Llansamlet there is even a Clarke Way named after him. One of the more remarkable features of life in the Lower Swansea Valley in the nineteenth-century period was the Victorian capacity for 'waste not – want not'. The various copperworks tried to waste nothing especially if some money could be saved or wrung from the exercise as a result. Many by-products were sold off either as building material, fertiliser or re-used in the copper-making process. One of the more remarkable was the requirement of the tenants living in the Grenfell housing at Taplow Terrace, Riflemen's Row and Grenfelltown that their very urine be saved for use in the copper pickling process. Although further research has indicated that it was unlikely to have been used for this purpose and was more likely to have been employed for its cleaning properties. I've often speculated on how the urine was collected and was told by Mrs Roach that one of her forebears, a Rebecca Evans, was involved in this perhaps most onerous of activities. Inevitably known locally as 'Becca Pee' she was born in 1881 and died in 1964 at the age of eighty-three. Family legend has it that as a young woman her job was to carry earthenware jars of urine to the copperworks after collecting it from local public houses etc. Again legend has it that they carried them on their heads. The local slang term for the urine was 'sig'. Alan Roach can remember being told by his mother that when she was a young girl she would take her father's food to Upper Bank at meal times. She also recalled beer being delivered from the Gwyndy Inn at Pentrechwyth. This was when the family lived at No. 1 Grenfelltown. Inevitably there is a family legend concerning the collection of urine and Alan Roach recounted one such story to me. A fellow worker of Harry Davies called Dai Hopkin fell into a large vat of urine during a shift at Upper Bank. As he hauled himself out of the sig an understandably very concerned Harry Davies asked him how he was. Dai Hopkin replied with his pipe still clenched firmly between his teeth, 'Yes Harry I'm alright, only my pipe has gone out'. Alan Roach's grandmother (Harry's wife) was Elizabeth Anne Thomas who was born near the Gwyndy public house in Pentrechwyth. When Harry retired through ill health she returned to her trade of dressmaker which she carried on from No. 1 Grenfelltown until Harry's death in 1946. Alan Roach described her as a powerful personality who negotiated the sale of No. 1 Grenfelltown from the owners of Upper Bank when Harry was forced to retire.

Going back to 'Becca Pee', she was a woman of many parts and had a wonderful singing voice singing in amateur opera. She was reputed to have sung for Madame Patti at Swansea's Albert

Two copper plates presented to
David John's family.

Two pages from the works log of David John, a stonemason at the Hafod Copperworks 1916-31. Near the top of the right-hand page can be seen an entry recording the visit of Prime Minister David Lloyd George (1863-1945) to Morriston in 1918.

Hall when it was still a theatre. Amazingly an image of her in old age has survived because she was painted by the artist John Cliel and it is reproduced in this book. 'Becca Pee' lived next door to Georgie Clarke, the last ferry man, in the Foxhole district of Swansea. Alan Roach recounted to me a fascinating story concerning Georgie Clarke:

During the Second World War my father was called up and my mother took over my father's insurance agency with Cooperative Insurance Services. The agency was based in the Hafod and my mother regularly used the ferry on the way to work. Sometimes I went with her collecting the premiums. This must have been in 1943 when Georgie Clarke was the Ferryman. We lived in Jersey Road Bonymaen and caught the bus from the Jersey Arms and travelled to lower Foxhole, crossed the railway line and went down the very slippery steps to the ferry. At this time Georgie had a small shelter, if I remember correctly, where he was able to 'brew up' (make tea) if custom was slack.

One story recounted to me by my mother was of her noticing a salmon at the waters edge and directing Georgie, who was in his boat, in the use of his oars to scoop the fish onto the bank where my mother was able to catch it. An earlier tale of the ferry was related to me by our neighbours in Bonymaen. People in the 1920's used to visit a shop in High Street which sold cheap furniture.

The ubiquitous 'Becca Pee' as painted by the artist John Cliel.

There was at this time no public transport to Bonymaen and women of the period were reluctant to walk through the docks area as it was a notorious red light district. Our neighbours' mother walked to the ferry crossed to the Hafod and made her way to High Street where she bought a table and proceeded back to the ferry carrying it on her head. The ferryman on her arrival explained that there was no room in the boat for her or her table. As a result of the subsequent forceful negotiations our neighbour's mother persuaded the ferryman to tow the table across the river with its owner sitting on board the table. The agreement was that if she or the table didn't make it there would be no payment. She did make it and carried the table on her head all the way from Foxhole to Bonymaen.

five

No 'Dark Satanic Mills'

This chapter was inspired by an article I read in the *New Scientist* magazine whilst sitting in my dentist's waiting room in 2005. It was written by an American academic called A. Bowdoin Van Riper, who is a member of the Social and International Studies Department at Southern Polytechnic State University, Marietta, Georgia. It is a 'what if' look at what the early stages of the Industrial Revolution might have been like had electric motors been available instead of steam-powered engines.

Needless to say Van Riper's counterfactual approach would have had profound implications for Swansea had electricity replaced steam as the driving force behind the Industrial Revolution in the period 1750 to 1850. There is, though, a central fallacy at the heart of his assumption that the early advent of cheap electric motors would have lead inevitably to industry and power generation being dispersed. An expert I consulted took the view that then as now, that power generation would be centralised in order to practise economies of scale. This would have enabled Swansea's longstanding coal-mining industry to both grow and find a market that would lie in supplying generating plants strategically dispersed throughout the region. The downside of this scenario is that the economic rationale behind bringing the copper ore from Cornwall to the coal supply and smelters at Swansea would also disappear. Then, as now, the smelting would be carried out in the ore fields themselves. It follows then that the tin and steel industries would not have needed to gravitate to West Wales. Instead they would almost have certainly chosen to locate nearer to markets in the large urban areas such as Cardiff, Bristol and Birmingham. All of which would have had spatial consequences for Swansea, especially for the outlying suburbs like Dunvant, Gorseinon and Clydach that grew up and around industries based close to them. Without the need for the Vivians or the Grenfells to build large smelting plants alongside the River Tawe there is no need to build 'Trevivian'/Hafod or the housing above Pentrechwyth. John Morris probably does not build 'Morris Town'. The North Dock is not built (1845-52) nor is South Dock (1852-59) so that area of town does not change because of the arrival of bigger vessels bringing more and more copper ore to Swansea. So would the 'Capehorners' of legend then have operated out of Cornwall instead of Swansea? Perhaps Gabriel Powell (1709-1789), steward of the Duke of Beaufort would then have been able to keep Swansea simply a picturesque medieval coal-exporting port with a thriving tourist industry. Perhaps Beau Nash (1674-1761) would not have left for London and ultimately Bath. Perhaps he would have stayed and formed a partnership with a decent local architect as he did in reality with John Wood Snr in Bath. Perhaps between them they might have built a Georgian seaside destination despite the lack of royal patronage that so favoured Bath and Brighton. Perhaps the arrival of the rail network at Swansea in 1850 would have worked to make the town more attractive to day trippers. Perhaps not. Unfortunately the main reason for running a railway line through South Wales then would have been to connect Fishguard with London providing the shortest route to Ireland. Such a line would probably run north of Swansea via Morriston with no commercial reason to run south to the mouth of the Tawe and the sea. As a result little if any resort development would have taken place at all. But for the sake of our little conjecture, let's say it did. Perhaps such a railway-driven tourism base would have sustained Swansea when the coal deposits began to deplete, as they would have done roughly at the same time as they did in reality. Although the demand for coal would not have run down quickly, there would undoubtedly have been an export dimension to assist this, presumably to France. Perhaps the 'Capehorners' would have become the 'Cornwallers' and been running down to Cornwall full of Welsh coal and coming back either in ballast or full of semi-finished copper goods destined for Bristol or Birmingham by train. Swansea's streets would have been lit by electricity in the 1770s rather than gas in the 1820s. In this scenario Swansea's population grows only very slowly and is sustained by the export of coal, its agrarian hinterland and tourism. The town grows to the north and west as it did in reality but at a far slower rate. It would not have been all good news, though. Agricultural workers in Pembrokeshire would not have been drawn in off the land as they were in reality. So perhaps the grinding poverty of subsistence farming would have stayed the norm. Consequently the crews of many a Swansea Capehorner would have been denuded of West Walian farm boys running away to sea. The fashionable area around the mouth of the Tawe might have expanded along the seafront heading west around the bay to the village of Mumbles and there would have been only modest docklands expansion to cope with the export of coal. Perhaps none at all. Perhaps they would have continued to load and unload from riverside wharves. In this scenario the Tawe is not straightened out by the New Cut and so Tyr Llandwr Farm on the east side does not disappear in the name of industrialisation. Without the copper industry and its toxic by-products, Kilvey Hill would still remain a wooded feature in the landscape. It might have retained its windmill and perhaps more would have clustered around it as 'clean energy' took over. It might have done this because its trees would not have been cropped for fuel nor poisoned by copper smoke; similarly the farms of Llansamlet would have remained workable. By retaining Kilvey Hill's trees, the topsoil would not have been washed off into the river further advancing deforestation. The copper smoke trials in the early part of the nineteenth century would not have happened. Perhaps even the prolific oyster beds at Mumbles might have survived a bit longer because of the lack of pollution coming down the Tawe and being disgorged into the bay. They would probably still be wiped out by disease and over-fishing, but perhaps they might have survived a decade or so longer as an industry. In my mind's eye I can see numerous oyster skiffs off Mumbles with elegant Georgian townhouses sprinkled around the arc of the bay with vividly coloured bathing machines admitting archaically clad bathers into clean waters. True, a steady stream of coastal trading vessels grimy with coal dust would scud in and out of the river seeking the Bristol Channel. They would be trading with France and a more heavily industrialised southern England, coming back full of merchandise for the thriving town-centre shops to sell to tourists and locals alike. It is a very seductive image, a 'green Swansea' without the pall of heavy industry hanging over it, thronged with tourists and a low-density population living in homes dispersed over a greater area. With those homes powered by a local electricity grid rather than hundreds of sooty coal fires. Swansea might have had a seasonal tourist trade comprised of the infirm and unwell coming to 'take the waters' and day trippers arriving by electric train from the by now heavily industrialised east of Wales. The rest would come by boat from Bristol and north Devon. Coal would still be mined as it had been done since the 1500s from outcrops further up the valley and this rather than copper would become the principal industry of the region. Nevertheless, Swansea would still have depleted its coal supplies and had to deal with the arrival of cheap flights to the Mediterranean resorts of the early 1960s. Perhaps like Porthcawl down the coast it might have survived an early industrialisation and gone on to convert itself into a regional holiday resort and flourished. Porthcawl came into being because of the availability of coal from the Lynfi, Garw and Ogmore Valleys and because Porthcawl was the nearest harbour, albeit a tidal one. Although in its heyday it was big enough to hold 100 ships, it crucially did not go on to develop 'floating docks' as did

A conjectural view of what Swansea might have looked like in the middle of the nineteenth century had the copper industry not arrived 100 years before. There are no docks as all vessels moor in the river and unload as the tide allows. They are loaded with coal mined further up the valley and brought to the town by canal. Without the copper industry Swansea would probably have remained a picturesque regional tourism resort with an extensive agricultural hinterland and an economy underpinned by the coal industry.

Llanelli, Cardiff and much later Swansea. Adding floating docks to a town increased greatly the number of ships that could be handled almost around the clock. What Porthcawl was successfully able to do was make the transition from industrial port to regional leisure resort. Immediately before and after the Second World War many inhabitants of the town can recall seeing double-decker buses full of miners and their families coming from the Rhondda to spend their 'Miners Fortnight' there. It was able to make this transition because, being primarily a coal-exporting port, it left little industry in its wake except some railway infrastructure. In reality Swansea's almost insuperable problem was the legacy of dereliction and pollution that the various metallurgical industries left behind them once deindustrialisation set in after the Second World War. If you can imagine those industries had never arisen then Swansea might have been Porthcawl as it were.

As you probably gather by now, counterfactual visions are fraught with ifs, buts and maybes. The sheer 'interconnectedness' of invention, science and industry means that if the industrial revolution had been electrically driven rather than steam driven then developments stimulated by the latter (improvements to boiler technology and the physics of steam production etc) would have retarded the development of the very electrical motors needed to make it work. The electric grid needed to supply a decentralised electricity network would then (as now) have needed massive supplies of coal. It would have also needed a fairly advanced degree of steam technology capable of converting coal into electricity at such power stations. As mentioned above, developments in copper go hand in hand with developments in steam – retard one and you retard the other. The other main problem with the counterfactual scenario is that it also has to ignore history. One of the key reasons the copper industry came to Swansea was that it had an abundance of cheap and easily accessible coal. That coal could be transported down to the town by a canal system built by local entrepreneurs. The Cornish copper masters could then set up works on land immediately adjacent to a river up which vessels full of copper ore could sail. Coal came down the valley by canal and copper came up the valley by river. At least until they built North Dock and then South Dock when it could then be transhipped to waiting rail wagons. The copper industry had begun in the region near Neath in the late 1500s and expertise and manpower had been accumulating (to say nothing of capital) ever since. For Van Riper's thesis to work you have to imagine that the many Cornish entrepreneurs who owned copper mines would then go on to ignore a trinity of locational virtues. Easy access to a navigable river via the Bristol Channel, cheap, accessible coal for the smelting process and a trained, compliant workforce. Unfortunately one has to keep backtracking through history to eliminate features that would enable an Arcadian non-industrialised Swansea thriving on tourism and exporting coal to come into existence.

One can only speculate what such a counterfactual scenario would have had on Swansea's 'urban elite'. After all in real life Swansea produced pioneer photographer Calvert Richard Jones, William Robert Grove ('father of the modern fuel cell') and the Royal Institution of South Wales also known as Swansea Museum. The latter held a conference in 1848 which attracted 847 of the UK's leading scientists; such was the town's status as an urban centre. Swansea also produced what has been called Wales's first modern newspaper, *The Cambrian,* the world's first passenger-carrying train (the Mumbles train) in 1807 and was home to the only branch of the Bank of England outside that country in 1826. The town also had a thriving professional and leisure class who had the time and money to indulge in pursuits like photography, the field sciences and natural history. That they were able to do this might be put down to Swansea's status as a resort town with a thriving industrial hinterland. Or because it was, as one historian recently put it 'a town with industry rather than an industrial town'. Ultimately Van Riper's counterfactual thesis works best against the background of the North of England's textile industry rather than Swansea's copper industry.

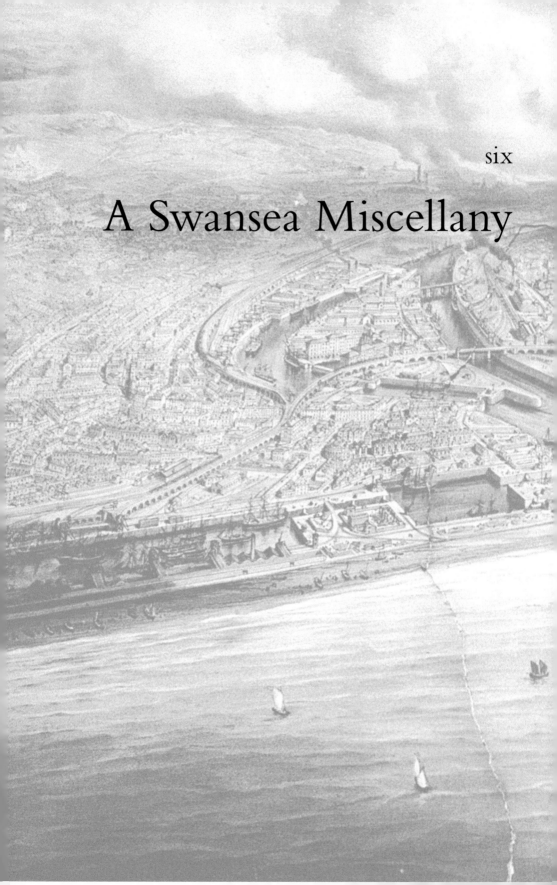

six

A Swansea Miscellany

A collection of dates, places, people and events from the twelfth century to the twenty-first.

1116 Attacks by the native Welsh on Swansea Castle by Gruffydd ap Tewdwr.

1150 More attacks by Rhys and Maredudd the sons of Gruffydd ap Rhys.

1188 Swansea is spelt 'Sweynsei' at this time.

1189 Attacked again by the Lord Rhys (Rhys ap Gruffydd) of Deheubarth.

1234 Swansea is mentioned in a Charter of Henry III.
The town's name is spelt 'Sweyneshole'.

1282 Wales was conquered by Edward I.

1326 Swansea Castle briefly became the centre of Edward II's royal administration.

1332 St David's Hospital is founded in Swansea on land very near to where the Cross Keys public house stands now.

1383 Construction begins of the Plas or Manor House in Castle Square. It was not demolished until 1840.

1404 Owain Glyndwr burns Cardiff to the ground.

1433 Swansea is spelt 'Sweynesey' in this year.

1463 Swansea is spelt 'Swaynesey' by now.

1536 The Act of Union divided Wales into counties, Cardiff was made the county town of Glamorganshire.

1546 Swansea's population stood at 900.

1553 By now it is spelt 'Swaunesey'.

1559 Cardiff is established as a port.

1585 The construction of a two-storey stone Guildhall or Court Room was begun in Swansea this year. The town stocks were located outside its main entrance and it was the seat of local government and justice until 1829, when a new Guildhall was built at Somerset Place.

1585 The town's name has evolved into 'Swansey' or 'Swanzey'.

1600 Swansea exported 3,000 tons of coal to Ireland.

1607 On 30 January a tide and wind-blown storm surge killed between 500 and 2,000 people in villages and farms along both sides of the low-lying Bristol Channel and Severn Estuary. These catastrophic inundations occur every 500-1000 years, on average.

1641 Swansea's population stood at 1,635.

1645 During the Civil War, Royalist Swansea was captured by the forces of Parliament.

1655 The first Quakers arrive in Swansea.

1674 Beau Nash, who later became Master of Ceremonies at Bath, was born in Swansea.

1682 Bishop Gore founded and endowed Swansea's first grammar school in this year.

1694 The Bank of England was established.

1695 It took 18 tons of coal to produce one ton of copper at this time.

1700 Swansea exported 18,000 tons of coal to Ireland.

1701 In this year Swansea exported almost 446 cwt of butter in ninety-two shipments of which the majority went to Plymouth.

1707 Swansea's population stood at an estimated 1,792.
It was easier in this year to transport coal 300 miles by sea than to transport it twenty miles overland by horse or pack mule. Most roads were nothing more than dirt tracks and turnpikes (an early and enterprising form of road pricing) which exacted a toll fee for access over private land.

1710 Gabriel Powell was born in this year. He was the Steward to the Duke of Beaufort and resisted most forms of harbour and town improvement.

1712 Between them (but acting separately) Thomas Newcomen (1663-1729) and James Watt (1750-1826) perfected the steam engine which energised (literally) the Industrial Revolution. Additionally, steam engines needed coal and many of their component parts made from copper. The need for the metal increases dramatically and Swansea was thus well placed to supply both.

1717 The first copperworks opened in the Swansea Valley at Landore.

1720 Daniel Defoe, the author of Robinson Crusoe, visited Swansea and described it as 'a seaport, and a very considerable town for trade, with a very good harbour'.

1722 In this year a vessel docked in Swansea carrying 200 casks of copper ore from New York.

1738 Swansea was spelt the modern way for the first time.

1740 Swansea was importing copper, grain and building ships.
      Richard Savage (1697-1743) was an eighteenth-century playwright and convicted murderer.
      A friend of Samuel Johnson (1709-1786) who later wrote his biography *The Life of Richard Savage*, the latter came to live in Swansea between January 1740 and the summer of 1741.
      Of the 116,000 quotations in *Johnson's Dictionary*, seven are from Savage.

1747 In this year 20,000 tons of coal was mined purely for metal smelting.

1750 The only building in what is now the Maritime Quarter was an inn.
      At this time Swansea was producing 50 per cent of Britain's copper.
      In this year it took 2,556 tons of coal to produce 243 tons of copper.
      John Vivian was born in Truro, Cornwall.

1757 The Upper Bank Copperworks was started by Chauncey Townsend and John Smith.

1760 John Wesley preached in the courtyard of the Plas House.

1764 The Cambrian Pottery was founded.

1768 Morris Castle (also known as 'the Graig') was under construction.

1786 The *Gloucester Journal* described Swansea as being 'in point of spirit and fashion, the Brighton of Wales'.

1788 Gabriel Powell the Duke of Beaufort's Steward and one of the most powerful men in Swansea in this period died in this year. He was born in 1710. He tried to stave off any development of the town that did not benefit his patron.

1790 The construction of Smith's Canal begins and follows the line of an old wagon way. It will carry coal from collieries in Llansamlet to coal staithes at Foxhole alongside the River Tawe. Coal staithes were early landing stages at which coal could be lowered via shutes into waiting ships or barges. The remains of some can still just about be seen on the east bank of the river opposite the former Unit Superheater Works.

1791 The Glamorganshire Canal was opened between Merthyr and Cardiff. It was the only means of conveying coal from the coalfields down to the port. The distance between Merthyr and Cardiff was twenty-five miles and the coal was carried in barges pulled by horses.

1793 William Jernegan built Mumbles Lighthouse for the Swansea Harbour Trust. This building can still be seen to this day and the light still operates, albeit using modern technology.

1794 The Swansea Canal Navigation Co. starts to build the Swansea Canal between Abercrave and Swansea.

1795 A high spring tide allied to a strong south-westerly gale produced a tidal surge that inundated the Burrows (Cambrian Place, Gloucester Place etc).

1798 The Swansea Canal was completed and ran for sixteen miles between Abercrave and Swansea; it was the M4 of its day in terms of commercial traffic. It connected the coal mines of the Upper Swansea Valley with the metallurgical industries of the Lower Swansea Valley and delivered coal for export. It was abandoned to dereliction in the period 1928-1962.

1801 Swansea's population stood at 6,821, Cardiff's was 1,870 and Merthyr's was 7,700.
In this year the Parys Mountain copper mine on Anglesey was the largest in the world.

1802 Admiral Nelson visited Swansea and was given the Freedom of the Borough on 12 August in this year.

1804 Sir John Morris informed the shareholders of the Oystermouth Railway or Tram Road Co. at the Bush Hotel on High Street (the building can still be seen) that a rail link would be created between Swansea and Mumbles. It would carry coal, limestone and minerals from Castle Hill to the Swansea Canal.
The pioneer photographer of early Victorian Swansea, Calvert Richard Jones, was born.
Thomas Williams (the 'Copper King') who owned the Parys Mine Co. died; he owned the Upper Bank and the Middle Bank Copperworks located alongside the Tawe in Swansea. These works merged to form Williams & Grenfell owned by his son Owen Williams, and Pascoe Grenfell.

1805 What has been called 'the first modern newspaper in Wales', *The Cambrian* was first published in Swansea in this year.
On 22 October of this year Admiral Lord Nelson died at the battle of Trafalgar; most (if not all) of his fleet had their hulls sheathed by copper made in Swansea.

1807 On 25 March, the Mumbles Train started carrying passenger traffic. It would be another twenty years before the Stockton and Darlington Railway came into existence. Until this date Mumbles could only be reached by walking along the beach at low tide.

1808 The Theatre Royal opened on the corner of Temple Street and Goat Street on 6 June.
The slave trade was abolished in the USA. Horseshoe-shaped copper bars called 'Manillas' were used as currency in the slave trade and Swansea copperworks manufactured these.

1809 Thatch is outlawed as a roofing material in Swansea.
The tin can is invented by an Englishman, although not perfected for mass production until 1846.

1810 The Hafod Copperworks was founded by John Vivian.
The world production of copper in this year was approximately 9,100 tons – by 1898 it would be 354,700 tons.

1811 Work started on Cambrian Place.
Swansea's population stood at 11,963.

1815 Wellington was victorious at Waterloo.
Swansea exported 108,000 tons of coal to Ireland in this year.

1817 The first steamer (the *Savannah*) crossed the Atlantic. She was an auxiliary powered vessel with paddles as well as sails, although she mostly used her sails for this voyage.

1818 Thomas Bowdler (1752-1825) completed his *Family Shakespeare* at his home overlooking Swansea Bay.

1821 Swansea's few streets were lit by gas.
Henry Hussey Vivian was born in this year; he would eventually come to manage the Hafod Copperworks after John Henry.

1826 The Bank of England decided to open a branch on Temple Street in Swansea in the face of competition from Merthyr, Cardiff and Liverpool. Birmingham and Manchester were the other towns chosen for branches.
John Vivian (born 1750), the founder of the Vivian copper dynasty, died in this year.

1830 Calvert Richard Jones donated a site for Swansea Market.
The Marquess of Bute obtained an Act of Parliament for the building of the Bute West Dock in Cardiff's docklands. Swansea was still twenty-one years from completing a similar floating dock (the North Dock).

1831 Swansea's population stood at 19,672, Newport's was 7,000.
In this year Cardiff was described as a 'small ill-looking Welsh village with a population of six thousand where most of the people were either fishermen or small farmers'.
The scientist Michael Faraday discovered electromagnetic induction, i.e. that electricity was induced in a copper wire when it was moved through a magnetic field. The way is paved for the electric motor, the generator and it freed electricity generation from the chemical battery. Copper's role in all this was crucial.

1832 Upper and Lower Union Streets built.
Morse invented the electric telegraph.

1835 Swansea became a borough with a mayor.

1836 The Swansea Borough Police Force established.

1837 Plymouth Street was built.

The Vetch Field was still called Fleming's Meadow.

Victoria succeeds to the Throne of England upon the death of William IV; the Victorian Age begins.

1838 Cholera outbreak.

Brunel's *Great Western* makes its maiden voyage from Bristol to New York in this year. It was totally steam driven and powered by a screw propeller not auxiliary paddles or sail.

1839 Cardiff's Bute West Dock was opened in this year and coal exports rose from 4,562 tons to 46,000 tons within a year.

Llanelli built its first 'floating harbour'. Despite the burgeoning copper trade, Swansea would take another thirteen years before building its first, the North Dock.

The Chartist uprising in Newport was quelled by the use of force.

In this year there were forty-six Welsh churches in the US.

1840 The 'New Cut' was started in this year. It was 840 yds long and between 55-70 yds wide. Work began in May and it took two hundred 'navvies' to excavate it.

In this year John Henry Vivian (1785-1855), the owner of the Hafod Copperworks, decided to allow his workers to work twelve-hour shifts instead of twenty-four-hour ones.

The penny post and the postage stamp (Penny Black and Two Penny Blue) were introduced on 1 May.

1841 The Royal Institution opens, now called Swansea Museum and the oldest in Wales.

Swansea's population stood at 19,115, Cardiff's was 10,077 and Merthyr's was 34,977.

1842 The excavation of North Dock began.

1843 The last cavalry charge on British soil occurred in Carmarthen in this year.

The 4th Light Dragoons charged a gathering of Rebecca Rioters.

1845 New Cut opened on 14 March.

The first tinplate works opened in Swansea Valley at Upper Forest.

In this year out of the 3,369 houses in the town only 470 had a water supply.

Most people still used wells, streams or street water vendors who sold it by the bucket with all the implications that had for hygiene.

H. H. Vivian is given general management of the Hafod Copperworks, aged twenty-five.

By now Vivian & Sons had agents acting for them in London, Liverpool, Birmingham, Glasgow, Belfast, Dublin, New York, Chicago, California and Canada.

1848 A mail coach leaving London at 8.55 a.m. would not arrive in Swansea until 1.00 p.m. the next day giving a journey time of virtually sixteen hours. Nowadays it takes three hours twenty-eight minutes by train or three hours by car.

The eighteenth British Association for the Advancement of Science conference was held at the Royal Institution of South Wales (now Swansea Museum) in this year, over 800 scientists attended. This was a tangible benchmark of Swansea's civic standing that an event of this kind could be held in a provincial town outside England.

Even without parliamentary approval the Marquess of Bute decides to press ahead with the construction of another large dock, the Bute East Dock. Swansea had yet to complete its first floating dock.

At Penllergaer, John Dillwyn Llewellyn (1810-1882) experimented with a boat powered by an electric motor.

1849 There was a cholera outbreak in Swansea.

In this year the town had seven to eight miles of streets but only as a few as 183 lamps with which to light them. Lighting was the province of a private sector company called the Swansea Gas Co. In addition the Swansea Water Co. supplied 924 houses with a mains water supply and their mains covered three-fifths of the town. The water pressure was described as uneven and irregular.

Morris Lane, known now as Kings Lane, was described in one health report of the time (George Clark's General Board of Health) as 'the dirtiest alley in the town'.

1850 Forty per cent of all Britain's iron output was being produced in South Wales. America produced roughly 1 per cent of the world's copper.

High Street Railway Station opened, the first South Wales railway train ran from Cardiff to Swansea on June 18.

The last mail coach ran from Cardiff to be replaced by a South Wales Mail service (2 August).

Housing in Sandfields began being built.

Dillwyn Street was built – then on the edge of town.

In September of this year the old ferry boat service from St Thomas to Swansea ceased operation upon the creation of a temporary footbridge.

The ferry service had been in operation for centuries.

On 18 June of this year Brunel's Landore Viaduct was opened, an estimated crowd of 20,000 looked on. A train arrived from Cardiff having taken two and a half hours – it now takes forty-five minutes by diesel Sprinter Train.

In 1850 it took three-and-a-half hours to get from Chepstow to Swansea by stagecoach.

1851 Swansea's population reached 19,672, Newport's was 19,000.

For the first time a bridge link existed between east and west Swansea.

According to the 1851 Census, just over 8 per cent of the population of Swansea had been born in Devon.

In Swansea during this year, 132 babies out of every 1,000 died in their first year.

In this year 44 per cent of Swansea's children aged five to fourteen went to school.

Before this year the River Tawe was the main source of drainage in Swansea apart from the town ditch. The first purpose-built drain was built in the town in this year and ran from East Burrows, along Pier Street, Adelaide Street and Victoria Road. It crossed to the Strand and went as far north as Morris/King's Lane.

In 1851 Swansea's principal imports were metallic ores, timber, tobacco, hemp, tallow, flour

Swansea at the apex of its maritime-industrial success in 1880. Access to the sea, a river navigable for several miles upstream and a position on the western edge of the South Wales coalfield all made Swansea a centre for the Victorian copper smelting industry. The docks, which came later, made the town into one of the great ports of the nineteenth-century world.

and grain. The principal exports were copper, iron, tinplate, coal, culm, patent fuel, alkali and earthenware.

The world's first underwater electric cable was laid between Britain and France. It used four copper wires, covered separately by gutta percha and lasted until 1875.

1852 North Dock is opened.
The excavation of the South Dock began.

1853 An electric telegraph link between Cardiff and Swansea was established.
Wales's first school of art was established at Swansea in this year and from 1887 occupied the top floor above the Central Library on Alexandra Road in a new building by Henry Holtom of Dewsbury.

1854 In this year there were seventy-six collieries operating in the various districts around Swansea. An economic rule of thumb in the nineteenth century was that the price of coal doubled for every two miles that it was transported from the colliery.

1855 Cardiff's Bute East Dock was partially completed.
John Henry Vivian died (born 1785).

1856 The end of the Crimean War.

A view above Swansea looking east at some point before the Second World War.

1858 Brunel's *Great Eastern* was launched.

1859 South Dock opened.
Cardiff's Bute East Dock is extended. Additional docks were opened there between 1874 and 1907 giving a total dock provision of 165 acres (66.8 hectares).

1860 Swansea's Union Workhouse was built at Mount Pleasant.
Swansea's first building bylaws were introduced.
During this decade Chile became the world's leading copper-ore exporter.
Between this year and 1872, some 80,000 Welsh people emigrated to the US. The majority went to the anthracite coalfields of Pennsylvania. Their daily rates of pay were often double what could be earned in Wales.

1861 Swansea Prison was built on Oystermouth Road, it was also known as 'Cox's Farm' after the name of the governor.
Swansea's population stood at 33,972, Cardiff's was 32,954 and Merthyr's was 49,794.
From this year on the largest occupational group in Swansea were not copperworkers but seamen manning the Cape Horn copper ore barques.
Cardiff's first public library opened in the Royal Arcade.

1864 The Albert Hall on De la Beche Street is built. This building can still be seen today and is a Listed Building.
Porthcawl Docks exported 17,000 tons of coal.

1865 On 9 September a sailing vessel (the *Hecla*) moored at the Cobre Wharf in the North Dock and her crew began unloading a cargo of copper ore brought from Cuba. During

Cradock Street in central Swansea at some point in the early twentieth century. Note the ornate design of the tram power poles.

the voyage three crew members had died of yellow fever and another was to die later in a lodging house in Swansea.

1866 The Statue of Liberty was assembled in New York City, it contained 80 tonnes of copper mined in Norway and was assembled by French workers.

1869 Swansea Hospital was built on open countryside along St Helen's Road, only a fragment now remains.

1871 Swansea's population stood at 51,702.
Porthcawl Docks exported 165,000 tons of coal in this year.

1872 In this year there were nearly 400 Welsh churches in the US.

1874 Horse-drawn trams began operating.
Cardiff opens the Roath Basin leading to the Roath Dock.
In this year 974 steam-powered vessels entered the port of Swansea carrying 248,502 registered tons of cargo as opposed to 4,222 steam ships which carried 531,262 registered tons.

1875 The Free Libraries Act was adopted in Swansea.

1876 Alexander Graham Bell invented the telephone; in America the transmission of voices was achieved via copper wires.

1877 The Pennsylvanian Welsh set up a colonisation society, the idea was to encourage fellow Welshmen to move from the industrial areas to the agricultural regions of the West.

1878 Excavation of the Prince of Wales Dock began.

1880 This decade sees the peak of copper imports to Swansea.
In this year there was one public house for every twenty-seven others in Swansea.
In this year the school leaving age was ten. It was only in this year that schooling for the five-to-ten year olds was made compulsory in the UK. It was done so in the face of much opposition from the poorer families who needed the income their working children provided.

1881 The Prince of Wales Dock opened.
Swansea's population stood at 76,430, Newport's was 35,000.
The Sunday Closing Act came into effect; public houses were closed on Sunday in this year.

1882 Britain invaded Egypt.
Construction of the Roath Dock began in Cardiff.

1883 Krakatoa exploded on 27 August in the South Pacific, the environmental consequences were felt globally.

1885 The demand for copper continued to grow with the invention of the internal combustion engine by Karl Benz in Germany. Many parts of the countless millions of cars to be made from this day forth would use components made of copper.

1884 In this year 2,248 steam vessels entered the port of Swansea carrying 836,405 registered tons of cargo as opposed to 2,706 sailing vessels carrying 343, 006 registered tons.

1886 Swansea Central Library & College of Art was built on Alexandra Road.
Swansea Art Society is founded by the Birchall family, it cost one guinea for working members, half a guinea for honorary ones and 5s for ladies.
Vivian & Sons employed 3,000 people, 1,000 of them at the Hafod Copperworks alone.

1887 The Swansea Royal Jubilee Metal Exchange was established.
The Roath Dock opens in Cardiff.

1888 This is the year in which the number of steam-powered vessels entering Swansea exceeded those of sail for the first time.
Glamorgan County Cricket Club is founded. It won the County Championship in 1948, 1969 and 1997. It also won the national league in 1993 and 2002 and enjoyed success in the one-day league in 2004 when it gained promotion to Division One of the County Championship.

Swansea's east and west pier was made of timber as can be seen in this postcard from the early twentieth century.

This is the South Dock looking west and full of coasting schooners and brigs in the 1880s.

1889 Barry Docks opened.
     800 vessels exported 227,000 tons of coal from Porthcawl in this year.

1890 The Royal Jubilee Metal Exchange became the business centre of the tinplate industry in the UK.
     Swansea exported 418,725 tons of tinplate this year.

Castle Square.   Swansea.

This is Wind Street in central Swansea. The Ben Evans department store can be seen at top left and the statue of Henry Hussey Vivian can now be found near St Mary's Church beside the Quadrant shopping centre.

1891 Swansea's population stood at 90,349.

In this year the American Senator William McKinley introduced the McKinley Tariff which was created to protect the embryonic American tinplate industry from foreign competition. It did this by increasing the cost of imported tinplate by seventy per cent. In 1900 McKinley became the second US president to be assassinated (Lincoln was the first).

1893 The school leaving age was raised to eleven in Britain.

1894 Henry Hussey Vivian died (born 1821).

Ben Evans department store opened on Castle Bailey Street.

In this year 2,805 steam-powered vessels entered the Port of Swansea carrying 1,357,429 registered tons of cargo as opposed to 1,726 sailing vessels carrying 253,856 registered tons.

1896 In this year William Grove the scientist and lawyer was born. He invented Grove's Battery in 1839, widely regarded as the 'father of the modern fuel cell' he became a QC in 1853, a judge in 1871 and was knighted in 1872.

Grove Place in Swansea was named after him. His family lived in a villa called 'The Laurels' where Swansea's Central Police Station now stands.

1898 Port Talbot Docks opened.

This is the North Dock on 2 October 1934. It is in dereliction by now having closed in 1931. It was the first of Swansea's 'floating docks' and was opened in 1852. Only the backs of the houses that overlooked the dock can still be seen.

1899 Queen Victoria celebrated her Diamond Jubilee.
The Boer War started on 11 October of this year and was to prove the most bloody conflict between Waterloo and the First World War that British forces would see action in.
The school leaving age was raised to twelve in Britain.

1900 This year represented the peak of refined copper imports to Swansea at roughly 70,000 tons per annum. By now America led the world in terms of copper production, it produced 60 per cent of total production.
Electric-powered trams began operating in Swansea.
Swansea exported 286,750 tons of tinplate in this year.

1901 Queen Victoria died at 6.30 p.m. on 22 January this year. Prince
Edward was made King. The Victorian era ended and the Edwardian era began.
At this time Swansea imported wood for making pit props from France, iron ore from Spain, lathwood from Russia, potatoes from Belgium, copper ore from Canada, steel bars from America and grain from Argentina. Swansea traded with the world.
Swansea's population was 94, 537, Cardiff's was 164,333 and Merthyr's 69,228.
The Mumbles Battery was equipped with two. 303-inch Maxim guns on either side of the fort beneath the lighthouse. The Maxim gun was invented by Hiram Maxim an American living in London it was the world's first single-barrel fully automatic machine gun.
In this year the Boer War was costing Great Britain £2,500,000 per month to prosecute.

1902 The Mond Nickel Works was established at Clydach, it still trades now but under the name of 'Inco'.

The Boer War ended in this year; a memorial to the soldiers who died in the conflict can still be seen on the promenade at Oystermouth Road. A total of 22,000 British soldiers died in this war.

1903 As a result of competition from Barry and Port Talbot, Porthcawl handled only 2,767 tons of coal this year.

1904 In this year 3,571 steam-powered vessels entered the Port of Swansea carrying 1,987,544 registered tons of cargo as opposed to 1,353 sailing vessels carrying 191,647 registered tons. By this year 6,000 ships passed through Cardiff with a tonnage of 8,234,000, London's was 7,890,947 and Liverpool's 6,730,262 tons.

In this year some 9 million tons of coal was exported from Cardiff Docks.

At the Elba Colliery at Gowerton a mining disaster claimed the lives of fifty miners.

1906 In Swansea at this time there were 58,777 monoglot English speakers.

Swansea's first council housing was built.

On June 27 in this year the town was rocked by an earthquake that measured 5.2 on the Richter scale.

1907 Swansea's corporation telephone service was sold to the National Telephone Co. on March 31 of this year.

In 1907, 1,999,688 tons of anthracite was exported from South Wales. Swansea contributed 1,761,687 tons, although little of it was mined in the Lower Swansea Valley.

1909 The King's Dock was completed.

1910 Richard Glynn Vivian dies (born 1835).

Swansea exported 482,981 tons of tinplate in this year. It went to Russia, Denmark, Germany, France, Portugal, Belgium, China, Java and the US

1911 Swansea's population stood at 152,619.

The Glynn Vivian Art Gallery was opened.

Edward George Bowen, the father of airborne radar, was born in Cockett.

1912 In this year part of Swansea Castle's north curtain wall (built in the fourteenth century) was dismantled so that the offices of the *Cambria Daily Leader* could be built.

Swansea Town Football Club was formed.

The world's first cheque for £1 million was written at the Coal Exchange in Cardiff.

The *Titanic* sank on its maiden voyage in this year.

1913 Swansea became the first Welsh football club to play in the FA Cup First Round.

Cardiff was by now the biggest coal exporting port in the world.

By this year four out of every five tinplate workers in Great Britain lived within a twenty-mile radius of Swansea.

In this year there were 106 tinplate mills in the Lower Swansea Valley.

At a colliery in Senghennydd 439 miners were killed in an underground explosion.

1914 Dylan Marlais Thomas was born at Cwmdonkin Drive in the Uplands.

The First World War began.

In this year 4,218 steam-powered vessels entered the port of Swansea carrying 2,877,619 tons of cargo as opposed to 888 sailing vessels carrying 128,764 tons.

1918 The First World War ended, 37,000 officers and 635,000 other ranks from all over the UK perished in this conflict.

The school leaving age was raised to fourteen in Britain.

1920 The Queen's Dock opened.

King George V laid the foundation stone of Swansea University in this year.

1921 The refining of copper ends at the Hafod and Morfa works.

Harry Secombe the comic actor and tenor is born 8 September in the St Thomas district of Swansea.

Swansea Town FC were elected to the Football League Division 3 (South) in the season 1920-1921.

The first woman professor at a British university was appointed at Swansea in this year.

1924 Hafod and Morfa Copperworks combined to form British Copper Manufacturers.

In this year 56.21ins of rain were recorded to have fallen on Victoria Park. This was 5.61ins more than fell in 1923. In 1921, 33.87ins of rain fell. The average for the last seventeen years was 49,166ins.

1926 Arthur Pendarvis Vivian died (born 1834).

1928 The North Dock was closed.

The Trades Union Congress was held at the Elysium Club on High Street.

1929 In this year the Local Government Act ended the Workhouse and Poor Law systems.

1930 The House of Lords rejects Sir Frank Brangwyn's (1867-1956) British Empire Panels. They were latterly housed in the Guildhall's Brangwyn Hall which was redesigned by the architect Percy Thomas to accommodate them.

In this year the US Census showed 60,205 foreign-born Welsh in residence, Pennsylvania had the largest number. Northern Pennsylvania had anthracite coal fields.

1931 Male unemployment in Swansea stood at 22.1 per cent – it was 12.7 per cent nationally.

The population of Swansea was 164,797 – Cardiff's was 226,937.

Even though a world recession was soon to set in, Cardiff exported 11 million tons of coal in this year.

1932 Swansea Town Football Club won the Welsh Cup for the first time in this year. It would do so again in the years; 1950, 1961, 1966, 1981, 1982, 1983, 1989 and 1991.

1933 Conservative politician Michael Dibdin Heseltine was born in Swansea in this year. In 2004 the *Sunday Times* Rich List voted him the 170th richest person in Britain.

1934 The Guildhall was built on St Helen's Road.

1935 Odo Richard Vivian died in this year (born 1875).

1936 Electric trams were superseded by motor buses in Swansea.

1939 The Second World War was declared on 3 September this year.
The writer Iris Gower was born in this year.

1940 In July of this year there were only three anti-aircraft guns sited in the whole Swansea area.

1941 Swansea city centre was bombed in the 'Three Nights Blitz' on 19, 20 and 21 February. In addition to 300 lives being lost, buildings destroyed include Ben Evans department store, the Three Lamps public house and the former Bank of England premises on Temple Street.

1942 As the War turned in favour of the Allies the Borough Engineer was instructed to make preliminary proposals for the reconstruction of Swansea after the War.
Ludwig Wittgenstein (1889-1951), arguably the most original and influential philosopher of the twentieth century and the author of *Tractatus Logico-Philosophicus*, came to Swansea in this year to recover from a gall-bladder operation.

1945 The Second World War ended.
The Health Service, Railway, Gas and Electricity industries were all nationalised in this year.
The Indian market for copper collapsed.

1946 The Mumbles Railway carried 4 million people in this year.
In this year the first Compulsory Purchase Orders were obtained under the 1944 Planning Act to enable the purchase of land at 1939 prices.
The average price of a house in the UK in this year was £1,459.
The philosopher Ludwig Wittgenstein spent his summer holidays in Swansea in this year and the next.

1947 A new Town and Country Planning Act repealed all earlier planning legislation. Each planning authority was now required to produce a development plan that included the reclamation objectives for derelict land.

The school leaving age was raised to fifteen in Britain.

1948 Sir Arthur Whitten-Brown died in Swansea in this year. With Captain John Alcock they were the first people to fly non-stop across the Atlantic in 1919. The flight left Newfoundland in Canada and arrived at Clifden in Ireland nineteen hours and twenty-seven minutes later. They won a £10,000 prize being offered by the *Daily Mail* and were knighted by King George V days after arriving back.

The writer Kingsley Amis (1914-1997) came to Swansea to take up a Junior Lecturer's post at the University of Swansea's English Department.

1950 The Kingsway was opened in November this year.

The present Archbishop of Canterbury, Rowan Williams, was born in Swansea in this year. He was educated at the recently demolished Dynevor School on Alexandra Road, now the site of Swansea Institute's School of Media Studies.

In this year there were already 2.3 million cars on the roads of Britain.

1951 In this year 24.9 per cent of Swansea's households lacked their own lavatory.

The population of Swansea was 160,988.

The pop singer Mary Hopkin was born in Pontardawe, she had a hit single in 1966 with *Those were the days.*

1953 In June of this year Castle Gardens was opened in time for the Coronation of Queen Elizabeth II.

1956 Gower was designated Britain's first Area of Outstanding Natural Beauty.

1957 The Swansea Parliamentary Committee asked the Minister of Works to de-list Swansea Castle as a scheduled ancient monument, to facilitate its demolition 'in the town's interests'. A campaign ensued which saw the castle acquired by the state and thus saved.

The Landore site (Hafod and Morfa works) was taken over by Yorkshire Imperial Metals, a joint firm of ICI and Yorkshire Metals.

1959 Colin Jones, holder of a Commonwealth Title, was born at Gorseinon in this year. He fought at Welterweight (147lbs or 667kg) He was a brave challenger for World Welterweight titles against leading American boxers and retired in 1982.

By this time there were 4.6 million cars on the road of Britain.

1960 The Mumbles Railway stopped running on 5 January his year.

Television licenses passed the 10 million mark for the first time in the UK.

The Editor of *Private Eye* and television panelist on *Have I Got News For You*, Ian Hislop, was born at Mumbles in this year.

1961   1.7 per cent unemployment in Swansea against a national average of 1.5 per cent.
       The Census in this year showed that over 14,000 dwellings in Swansea lacked hot water, a
       bath or an inside WC.
       The population of Swansea was 167,322.
       In May of this year the Dragon Hotel was opened on the Kingsway.

1963   Unemployment rate in Swansea was 3.8 per cent against a national average of 2.5 per cent.
       In this year 20 per cent of the dwellings in the city had been built before 1875.
       Television producer and writer of the current *Dr Who* series Russell T. Davies was born in
       Swansea. He was recently voted the seventeenth most powerful person in British television
       drama.

1964   The Ford Motor Co. came to Swansea in this year.
       Cardiff docks stopped exporting coal in this year.
       As recently as 1964/5 coal mines in the Swansea area produced in excess of two million tons
       of coal with 6,275 men employed in the pits (excluding management and admin people).
       This made the National Coal Board the largest employer of male labour west of Neath.
       By contrast British Rail employed 475,000 people in the UK as a whole.

1965   The unemployment rate in Swansea was 2.6 per cent against a national average of 1.4 per
       cent.
       Rob Brydon the actor and comedy writer was born in Swansea in this year, although he
       grew up in Baglan near Port Talbot.

1966   On 21 October in this year, 144 children and adults lost their lives in the Aberfan tip disaster.
       In the wake of Aberfan the Secretary of State for Wales announced the creation of a special
       unit to speed up the process of dealing with derelict land. Along with the introduction of
       a new Industrial Development Act which redesignated Swansea as a Development Area,
       this enabled the town to qualify for financial assistance when reclaiming derelict land.
       The population of Swansea was 168,790. Cardiff's was 253,920.
       On September 8 this year, the first Severn Bridge was opened.

1967   On 13 September the first element of grant aid (£129,000) was received from the Secretary
       of State for Wales to pay for the reclamation of the White Rock Tip. Some 85 per cent of
       this came from the Welsh Office and it signalled the beginning of the end of dereliction
       in the Lower Swansea Valley.
       The poet Vernon Watkins died in this year (born 1906), he worked at the St Helen's Road
       branch of Lloyds Bank for forty-one years until 1966.

1968   Malcolm Nash was hit for six sixes in one over by Gary Sobers in the Glamorgan v
       Nottingham cricket match on 13 August at St Helen's.
       Television Wales & West (TWW) lost its franchise to make commercial television
       programmes for that region. It was replaced by Harlech Television.

1969 Swansea was made a city in December of this year.
South Dock was closed to commercial traffic and was bought by the council.
The North Dock began to be infilled.
The actress Catherine Zeta Jones was born 25 September in this year.
Glamorgan won the County Championship in this season. Malcolm Nash was the most successful bowler with seventy-one wickets at an average of 18.98 runs. He also scored 435 runs at an average of 22.89 per game.

1970 In this year the number of cars on the roads of Britain had risen to 12 million.

1971 The last zinc works, the Imperial Smelting Corporation's Swansea Vale Works, closed in this year.
Fifty-four per cent of Swansea's households were owner-occupied in this year.
The painter Ceri Richards died in this year (born 1903). He was Wales' most significant painter of the mid-twentieth century and was born in Dunvant.

1972 The school leaving age was raised to sixteen in Britain.

1974 Plans for converting the South Dock and environs into the award-winning Swansea Maritime Quarter began to be drawn up.
Local government was reorganized. Swansea was dissolved as a County Borough (it had been one since 1898) and a new two-tier system was introduced whereby West Glamorgan County Council was created, as was Swansea City Council.

1975 The Welsh Development Agency was established in this year under the WDA Act. Its aim was to supply grants for 'derelict, neglected or unsightly land'.
Footballer John Hartson was born in Trallwn. He played for Luton, Arsenal, West Ham, Wimbledon, Coventry, Celtic and West Bromwich Albion before retiring in January 2008. He also played fifty times for Wales.

1976 In this year the average cost of a new house in Wales was £10,703 and £9.910 for an old one.

1978 The Leisure Centre was opened by HM The Queen in this year. It is a 102m x 63m rectangle and was built to a three-metre grid.

1979 The unemployment rate in Swansea was 7.0 per cent against a national average of 6.6 per cent.

1980 Yorkshire Imperial Metals ended copper production at Swansea.

1981 Population stood at 186,589 in this year. Swansea's Enterprise Zone was designated on 11 April

1986 Kingsley Amis won the Booker Prize for *The Old Devils,* which had a Swansea setting.

1987 It is estimated that tourism contributed £38 million to the local economy.

1990 The Driver Vehicle Licensing Agency (DVLA) was established. It employs over 7,000 people, of which 6,000 are full-time jobs. Its job is to maintain a record of the people entitled to drive one of the many millions of vehicles at large on the roads of Britain.
The Maritime Quarter (MQ) was Highly Commended in the European Urban and Regional Planning Awards.
The British Urban Regeneration Association gave the Maritime Quarter a Best Practice Award for an outstanding contribution to urban regeneration.

1992 The River Tawe Barrage was completed, the first in Wales.

1997 The footballer Ivor Allchurch died in this year (born 1929).

1998 The Welsh Industrial Maritime and Industrial Museum was closed in Cardiff Bay to make way for retail development, Swansea would eventually be chosen as its new home.

1999 In this year the Welsh Water Treatment Works on Fabian Way was given a Planning Achievement Award from the Royal Town Planning Institute.

2000 The Royal Institute of Chartered Surveyors gave the Welsh Water Treatment Works on Fabian Way a Building Efficiency award.
The number of cars on the roads of Britain had reached 24 million.

2001 In Swansea only seven babies out of every 1,000 died in their first year.
The first Technium 'business incubator' building was opened in Swansea by Welsh billionaire Sir Terry Matthews; it was oversubscribed in terms of companies wanting to become tenants even before opening.
Harry Secombe died on 11 April.
The average life span for males in Swansea in this year was seventy-five years and eighty years for women.

2003 Swansea became home to the National Swimming Pool when a new Olympic-sized facility was built at Ashleigh Road.
An estimated 9,000 people were self-employed in Swansea during this year, 8.9 per cent of the working population. This is 3 per cent lower than for the rest of Wales (12.5 per cent) and the rest of the UK (12.6 per cent).

2004 Redevelopment of the former Prince of Wales Dock (built 1878-81) commenced as a residential/leisure project called 'SA1'.
The second Technium 'business incubator' building opened in Swansea.
Weekly full-time earnings in Swansea are £383.00 against a UK average of £422.10.
The Swansea-born footballer and sporting legend John Charles died (born 1931).

2005 Unemployment in Swansea stood at 2.4 per cent; this rate is now in line with the national average of 2.4 per cent.

The National Waterfront Museum, Swansea opened on Victoria Road in October of this year and attracted 200,000 visitors in its first year.

Swansea was home to 7.6 per cent of the population of Wales. The population stood at 224,600 people in the city and county area; in 1801 it was 19,704.

In June of this year the rising price of metal (i.e. zinc, copper and lead) led to the restarting of mining on Parys Mountain on the north coast of Angelsey. One of Swansea's earliest sources of copper ore in the nineteenth century. The project is forecast to not only create jobs but act as a stimulant to heritage tourism in North Wales.

The Vetch Field home of Swansea Football Club for over ninety years closed and the club's new home became the Liberty Stadium at Morfa.

There were: 15.88 assaults, 18.62 burglaries 0.65 robberies per 1,000 of the population of Swansea

Swansea City Football Club achieved 67.8 per cent of capacity for home games while Cardiff achieved 57.0 per cent.

In this year Swansea had 1.25 million visitors who spent around £180 million an additional 2.2 million day trippers brought a further £58 million to the city.

2006 Eighty-six per cent of all local employees now work in the service/public sector. 7.2 per cent work in construction, 13.7 per cent work in manufacturing.

Swansea University has a student population of twelve thousand and is ranked among the top forty universities in the UK. It began life with just eighty-nine students in 1921 and was the twenty-ninth university to be established in the UK.

One third (33.3 per cent) of households were owned outright.

The global price of copper had tripled since January 2005. It was by now around $8,000 per tonne – it was $1500 in December 2001. The Chinese construction boom was cited as being used as one reason for the increase. There was also a damaging strike at one of Chile's largest copper mines which upset the global market for the metal.

Swansea Art Society celebrated the 125th anniversary of its founding in November 2006. It is the oldest in Wales.

Swansea Council manages 14,000 properties, making it one of the largest landlords in Wales.

Approximately 19 per cent of all retail enterprises in Wales are to be found in either Cardiff or Swansea.

2007 Oxwich Bay near Swansea is named the most beautiful beach in Britain and one of the best in the world by *Travel Magazine*.

Three-and-a-half million tourists visit Swansea annually; one of the main reasons given is the many beaches to be found nearby.

NASA announces that the universe is 13.7 billion years old.

2008 Swansea City Football Club are promoted from League One to the championship.

Other local titles published by The History Press

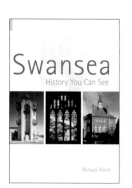

Swansea: History You Can See
RICHARD PORCH

The history of landmarks such as the Lockgate sculpture in Ferrara Quay, the copperworkers' township Hafod and the Whitford Point lighthouse - the only wave-washed cast-iron lighthouse in Britain – is recorded in this A-Z of the people, buildings, industries and events that have shaped the city and county of Swansea.

978 07524 3076 8

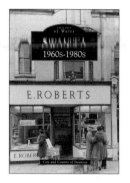

Swansea 1960-1980
CITY AND COUNTY OF SWANSEA

This impressive collection of photographs documents the changing face of Swansea during the latter half of the twentieth century. Drawn from across thirty years this comprehensive record captures an evolving city through the lens of the planners, councillors and academics directly involved in the transformation of Swansea. From its heavily industrialised origins, the reader is taken back in time to watch as the face of Swansea is altered by earlier wartime bombing and rebuilt through the redevelopment of derelict land into a lively and prosperous city.

978 07524 2456 9

Swansea at War
SALLY BOWLER

This book is an account of Swansea's experiences during the Second World War, as well as a tribute to all those in the town who kept Swansea's spirit alive through these dark days. Weaving together many personal accounts of the war years, most of them appearing in print for the first time, the author skilfully calls this period back into existence for those who remember these life-changing events, and provide a window onto a lost world for those who don't.

978 07509 4464 9

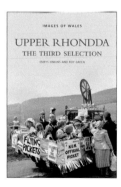

Upper Rhondda: The Third Selection
EMRYS JENKINS

This valley played a crucial role in the shaping of modern Wales through the imagination of its engineers and the toil of those who worked underground. All aspects of everyday life are recorded, from shops and churches to work and leisure. Its landscapes and landmarks are captured in this valuable historical record of life in the Upper Rhondda as it used to be and the changes that have taken place.

978 07524 37844

If you are interested in purchasing other books published by The History Press, or in case you have difficulty finding any History Press books in your local bookshop, you can also place orders directly through our website

www.thehistorypress.co.uk